Arabian Fairy Tales

About the Author

Amina Shah is the daughter of the illustrious Afghan man of letters, Professor the Sayed Ikbal Ali Shah, Khan. Her forebears, as Khans of Paghman, have been settled in Central Asia for centuries. Her father took his daughter with him on many of his journeys to Europe and Central Asia and since then she has travelled the world over, collecting tales of folklore such as these.

Educated both in England and in the East, she went to the Slade School of Art and published her first novel at the age of 19. Details of some of her books appear on p.207 et seq. Today she devotes much of her time to raising money for the Afghan refugees.

Amina Shah is chairwoman of the College of Storytellers, the British organisation which aims at encouraging storytellers and stimulating and reviving the ancient art of storytelling.

Arabian Fairy Tales

retold by

AMINA SHAH

For further information on
Sufi Studies please write to:
The Society for Sufi Studies
P.O. Box 43
Los Altos, CA 94022

THE OCTAGON PRESS
LONDON

ISBN 0 863040 48 9

First Published in this Edition 1989

Printed and bound in Great Britain by
The Camelot Press Ltd., Southampton

Contents

v

Introduction

THESE STORIES have been collected over a number of years, during travels which I have taken through all the Arabic-speaking lands.

At the time when most of these tales were first told, "Arabia" meant a very large area wherever Arabic was spoken; now, of course, many parts of ancient Arabia have different names. Saudi Arabia, known to us as the home of oil-sheikhs and the place where thousands of Moslems from other countries go on the pilgrimage to Mecca, is only one part of Old Arabia.

From earliest times the Arabs have been interested in story-telling. Some tales have a moral tone, others are purely for entertainment. Others had beginnings in the nomad tents, around camp fires in the desert, before the Arabs came to live in cities.

Even today, in countries where the Arab influence was strong (like the East African coast, Zanzibar, Morocco and Spain), the love of telling stories in public still exists. In many cases, plots, names and locale have been handed down in families for generations.

On Friday, the Moslem equivalent of the European Sunday, people often have not much to do once they have prayed in the mosque, or visited the colourful shopping area of their own district. Or they may be far away from home, travelling in deserted regions where they have to make their own entertainment.

The telling of a story is the purest art form these simple people know. To them the hosts of Jinn, Geni or Efrits are also part of their heritage, all around them in the atmosphere, invisible but capable of appearing at any moment.

There are great numbers of Jinn, or Geni, for there are said to be forty troops in existence, each troop consisting of six hundred thousand! They are reputed to be composed of fire, and if they are killed (not all of them are immortal) the fire in their veins consumes them until they are reduced to ashes. Their king and ruler is Suliman, Son of David (King Solomon in the West), and no man has ever gained such power over them. There are both good and bad Jinn, and the good ones stand at the right hand side of King Suliman's throne, while the bad ones are on the left. (It is strange, if we are looking for comparisons, that the Demon King or bad characters in pantomime always enter 'Left'!)

Jinn often carry away a human being, or show him (or her) where buried treasure lies; or (as in the case of Sinbad the Sailor) leap upon his back and stay there.

It is believed that the chief abode of the Geni are the Mountains of Kaf, which the ancient Arabs thought encircled the whole earth. At that time, with a lot of other people, they believed that our world was flat.

Wherever the Arabian language is understood, there will be found the stories which are included in this anthology. Some are about animals, which call to mind the fables of La Fontaine, others are similar to the tales of Grimm and Hans Andersen, because, in some way, all have a common root.

Children born in Mecca, Syria, or the southern part of the Hadramaut, know the same stories about princes who were turned into animals or monsters by magic, or poor peasants whose lives were transformed by sudden good fortune brought about by a talisman or a Jinn. Classical Arabian literature holds many of the finest stories in human knowledge, but the tales told by firelight, or starlight, or by the modern electric light bulb in coffee-houses of the present day from Cairo to Khartoum, from Andalucia to Nejd, show the imprint of many generations of constructive thought. This story-telling is a living craft, passed continually from grandparents to grandchildren, right down to our own day; from the time of Saladin and Haroun Al Raschid of Baghdad to the moment when you are reading this.

It will be noticed that seven is a magic, mystical number. Seven sons, seven daughters, feasts lasting seven days and seven nights, all have a repetitive pattern in these tales. Also "Allah sent them many sons" is as usual an ending to a story in the East as, "They lived happily ever after".

I have written of Caliphs and Sultans, Viziers and slaves, Jinn, Efrits, and the marvellous happenings of days long ago which concerned them. These are only a very small percentage of the stories being told in the souks (bazaars) and market-places wherever more than two people have half an hour to spare either to tell or listen. Arabia is the magic land of "Inshallah!" (If Allah wills) and so, with the Blessings of Allah, I leave you to read these stories yourself.

This book is dedicated to
the children of my brothers

The Sultan and the Four
Strange Brothers-in-law

ONCE UPON A TIME there was a Sultan who had four sons and four daughters. When he became very old he sent for his sons, and said to them:

"I want you to take notice of these words of mine, because I know I am soon to die."

"When I am no more whichever of you watches three nights in succession beside my grave shall be Sultan after me. Look after your sisters, and give them to the first who shall ask for them, no matter what they are. May Allah guide you, blessings upon you!"

So, having made his peace with all, the old Sultan died.

When he was buried, the eldest son went to sleep beside his father's grave. But at midnight there were such groans and moans in the graveyard that the young man was terrified out of his wits and fled home before daylight.

The next night, the second son, taking his prayer rug, waited there on his knees. But when it was pitch dark, hideous screams came from the tombs around. The second son took to

1

his heels and fled.

The night after that, the third son, thinking himself much braver than his brothers, was sure that he would be able to stay there for three nights.

Just before dawn, when the cocks were beginning to crow, a fit of shivering seized the young prince. He heard shrieks of ghoulish laughter all around him, and he ran back to the palace as his brothers had done.

The youngest brother, Ahmad, taking a sharp sword, went to watch beside the old Sultan's grave that night. Just before dawn he was startled by a most unearthly cry coming from behind the graveyard wall. A tremendous ghoul with burning eyes and semi-human form came at him with outstretched claws. The prince cut off its head with one lightning movement. Then he cut off its ears and put them in his pocket.

The cock crew, and it was morning, so the prince returned to the palace.

That night he returned to the graveyard, and at the early hour of dawn an Efrit appeared to him, with a fearsome head and teeth like a shark. With one blow he cut off its head, chopped off its ears, and put them in his pocket. As it died, the Efrit was reduced to ashes, from its own inner fire, for Efrits are consumed by this when they die.

The third night, he waited until the dawn, and then a most hideous Jinn, with folded arms and long hair, appeared. With one movement, the Prince cut off its head, and chopping off its ears, put them into his pocket.

Then, he returned to the palace and everyone declared that he was the new Sultan.

Some time later, a lion arrived at the court, and asked for the hand of the eldest princess.

"How can I give my sister to a lion?" cried the new Sultan, but the lion answered, "It was your late father's wish, was it not, that your sisters were to be given to the first who asked?"

And the Sultan agreed, so the lion took the princess away.

Time passed, and a leopard came to the court and asked for the hand of the second princess. So, as it was their father's last

2

wish that each should go to the first who asked for them, the second princess went to the leopard and he took her away.

No sooner had the leopard gone, than a gigantic eagle came and asked for the third sister. Regretfully, the Sultan had to let her go. Now there was only the youngest princess left.

"Perhaps," thought Sultan Ahmad to himself, "I shall be able to marry my youngest sister to a human being. Surely at least one of my sisters will be able to have a normal life and be happy in her marriage."

But no sooner had another day passed, before a huge Efrit, dressed in fine clothes, and with a ring on every finger of his hairy hands, came and asked for the fourth princess.

The poor princess shrank behind her brother's throne, and would have clung to it with all her strength, but the Sultan said:

"Sister, you must go, for did not our father (of happy memory!) tell us with his last breath to give you girls to whomsoever asked first for you?"

So the Efrit put the girl on his broad shoulders and flew off with her.

All the people of the country mourned their princesses as if they were dead, for soon the story of their strange marriages got to the ears of everyone.

And no one was more sorry than the Sultan. All day he attended to the affairs of state, but his heart was as heavy as lead.

The Palace was quiet after the four princesses had gone, and there seemed to be no laughter there or frivolity of any kind.

After a time, the Sultan longed for a wife, so that he could be happy.

Now, living by herself in a castle in the mountains, there was a beautiful girl called Kadijah.

Her father and mother were dead, and she had no relatives in the world.

On the wall of her bedroom was a golden mirror which had once belonged to her aunt who had been a Wise Woman. Each

3

day she looked into the mirror and said:

"Mirror, mirror, who will marry me?"

And the mirror answered:

"The wife of a sultan shalt thou be."

Sighing, Kadijah turned away from the mirror, wondering where in the world she would meet a sultan.

One day, she sent for her old nurse and said:

"Mother, let us go upon a pilgrimage, for I am getting sad and lonely here in the castle. We shall take one or two servants, and set off the day after tomorrow. Sew some pieces of gold into coarse garments such as simple people wear, and we will escape the attention of robbers that way. The journey to Mecca will bring me peace, I am sure."

By a curious coincidence, Sultan Ahmad and his Vizier decided to go on the pilgrimage at about the same time, so that it was not long before they met Kadijah and her servants on the road.

"Let us join the party of this humble family," said the Sultan, to the Vizier, trotting his horse up to Kadijah's small group. "It will give us some protection from brigands if we are all together."

The Vizier rode up to the litter where Kadijah reclined, and saying that he was the servant of a merchant making the pilgrimage, asked her permission, through the curtains, to join forces.

Kadijah willingly gave consent, and soon they were travelling together in the greatest harmony.

Of course, the men were not able to see Kadijah, veiled as she was, but peering through the curtains, she saw the Sultan, and was delighted with his good looks.

When they finally arrived at the Holy City and put up at an inn, Kadijah let her veil fall for an instant, and Sultan Ahmad fell in love with her at once.

But he dismissed her from his thoughts at the time, thinking that after all he was on the pilgrimage, and should be thinking only of spiritual things in Allah's House.

When they had both performed the necessary ceremonies, going

4

to Mount Arafat to stone the Devil's Pillar, and visiting the Tomb of the Prophet at Medina, they returned by the same road to their own homes.

Then said the Sultan to his Vizier: "My friend, I have fallen in love at first sight. I will marry this lady or no other. Go to her female attendant and find out her history, and report back to me."

"I hear and obey," said the Vizier, and spurred his horse. He spent some time riding beside the litter of the old nurse, and then came back to the Sultan.

The whole of Kadijah's life story was told, and to finish the Vizier said, "Mighty Sultan, the lady has a magic golden mirror which prophesies that she will become a Sultana!"

"Inshallah, by the Will of Allah, so she shall!" cried Ahmad, and made up his mind that, as soon as he had said his morning prayers, he would speak to the beautiful Kadijah himself about marriage.

Lying down beside the fire of camel-thorn, which the servants kept alight all night, he fell deeply asleep.

Now, no sooner had he done so, than a terrible storm arose.

Thunder, lightning, and sheets of rain threw the small camp into disorder.

The wretched pilgrims were soaked to the skin, their belongings blown away by the wind.

Kadijah twisted her ankle, the nurse was crying with cold, and the Sultan sheltered them with his cloak. The Vizier and the servants were trying to catch the horses, but they had no luck; the animals bolted and were soon out of reach.

"What can we do?" cried the nurse. "If we do not die of cold, then robbers will kill us!"

"Do not worry," said Kadijah, "I have a magic talisman here which my mother left me." She rubbed a star-shaped piece of metal hanging round her neck. "In the Name of Suliman, Son of David (upon whom be peace!), let us be rescued!"

There was a sudden sound as of a clap of thunder, and an Efrit appeared. It was none other than the one which had married the sister of the Sultan.

5

"I shall carry you to my home, you will be safe there," said the Efrit.

They all felt themselves being drawn up into the air, and landed in a sunny valley, where there was a fine house.

There, surrounded by the greatest luxury, the Sultan found his fourth sister.

"Peace be upon you, brother," said she. "Welcome to our home."

"Are you happy, sister?" asked the Sultan. "How does your husband treat you?"

"I am wonderfully happy, and I could not ask for a more affectionate and kind husband," replied the princess. "Although he is so fearsome-looking, he is gentle and good."

"Allah be praised!" said Ahmad. "I wish that I knew the same about our other three sisters."

"The one who married the lion is not far from here,'' was the answer. "Will you not go and visit her?"

Sultan Ahmad, after saying good-bye to the Efrit and his wife, set off once more. Kadijah had been given new clothes and so had all the members of the party, so they were not ashamed of their appearance when they got to the Lion's house.

"Welcome! Welcome!" cried the Lion when he opened the door. "Your sister is well, brother Ahmad, and you must stay here with us as long as you like."

While they were staying at the Lion's home, the Sultan asked the Lady Kadijah to be his wife, and she agreed. One night, while a great feast was in progress, the Sultan and she were married, and the prophecy of the magic mirror became true.

After three days of rejoicing, they decided they should continue the journey; so the Sultan went to the Lion, and said: "Good brother-in-law, thank you for all your hospitality, and the wedding feast; it has been a most happy time. If there is ever anything I can do for you, please ask, and it shall be done."

"There is only one thing which you could do for me," said the Lion, "and that is to help me to return to my human shape." But I do not suppose that you have the ears of a ghoul which I could throw into the fire, and thus break the spell which binds me?"

6

"Why did you not ask before?" said the Sultan, "I have the ears of a ghoul in my pocket. When I was watching beside my father's grave I killed one, and cut off its ears as I knew they were useful in magical rituals."

So the Lion lit a fire, threw the ears of the ghoul into it, saying a secret word, and was turned into a young and handsome man before Sultan Ahmad's eyes.

The Sultan's sister was delighted with her new husband, and sent the travellers on their way with many blessings.

When several days had passed, Ahmad and his Sultana came to a huge palace with great iron gates. Upon the castle wall was painted a design, that of a black leopard with white spots. When the gate-keeper opened the door, the Sultan asked for shelter for his wife and himself, the old nurse and the servants, until next day.

"My master, the Leopard, will come to you immediately," said the housekeeper, showing them into a large room hung with tapestries.

"The Leopard?" said Ahmad to Kadijah. "This must be where my second sister lives, for it was a Leopard who took her for his wife."

As he spoke, the Leopard entered the room and bade them welcome, saying, "My dear brother-in-law, how nice to see you! You must stay with us as long as you can; your sister has been waiting for news of you all for months."

Ahmad told him the story of their adventures after going on the pilgrimage, and the Leopard was amazed at the story of the Lion turning into a man again. "If only I could also become human once more," said the Leopard. "I was put under a spell by my wicked stepmother, and there is only one way to help me."

"And what is that?" asked Ahmad.

"The ears of a Jinn, thrown into a bucket of salt water," said the Leopard. "But where am I to get them?"

"I have the ears of a Jinn in my pocket," said the Sultan, and when the Leopard brought a bucket of salt water, he threw them into it. The Leopard said a magic word, and the next moment the leopardskin was lying on the floor. There stood a handsome

7

young man, who clasped his brother-in-law's hand, and called down the blessings of Allah upon him for helping him to regain his human shape. The princess was delighted with her new husband, and a feast was prepared which lasted three days and three nights.

Soon the Sultan and his Sultana set off on their travels again. They reached a lonely gorge where there was an eerie silence. This time they were dressed in the finest clothes, which the prince who had been a leopard had given them as presents, and even their horses had silver ornaments. "We are not more than a day's ride from our own country, O Sultan," said the Vizier, as they trotted along, "but I fear we might fall in with robbers in this desolate spot!" No sooner had he spoken, than they were surrounded by ten horsemen who appeared from behind the rocks. With bloodcurdling cries, the horsemen rode round the little party, waving ugly-looking knives. The Sultan and the Vizier drew their swords, and bravely defended the Sultana and her nurse. The four litter-bearers were huddled together with fear. Suddenly, out of the sky, came a gigantic eagle. It landed on the head of the robber chief, and flapped its wings in his face. The robber lashed out with his knife, but the eagle wrenched it away with its beak. Out of the sky came another eagle, and another, until the gigantic birds drove the robbers away, tearing at their clothes with their beaks.

The eagles then flew off, with the exception of one great bird, which Sultan Ahmad recognised as the eagle which had married his sister.

"A thousand thanks for saving our lives, brother-in-law Eagle," said the Sultan, and he told him everything which had happened since he went on the pilgrimage.

"If only I too, could be turned into human shape again," said the Eagle, "but the wicked witch who transformed me said that only if I were to carry the ears of an Efrit in my pocket, would I become a man again."

"But I have the ears of an Efrit, here, look, in my purse," said Ahmad, and he handed them to his brother-in-law. No sooner had the eagle's claw touched the purse, than he was changed into his own shape once more. So the spell was broken, and he took them to his house which was nearby. There the Sultan met his sister again, and she prepared a huge feast in honour of her husband's transformation.

After three days of jollity, they all said good-bye to each other, and at last Sultan Ahmad took his bride back to his own country.

The Sultan's people gave them such a welcome that there was rejoicing for a whole month, and they lived happily together until Allah sent for them at last.

The Peasant,
the King and the Sheikh

ONCE UPON A TIME a certain Persian came to the city of
Cairo to pit his wits against all the wise men of the royal court,
for he said that he was a learned vizier in his own land.

So the King of Egypt sent for him and, because of his reputation, raised him to a high position at court.

Then the great men of Al Azhar, the Golden University of
Islam, came and said to the King:

"O Great Shadow of Allah upon Earth, Gateway to Wisdom
and Jewel of the World, let this foreigner ask us a question
which we cannot answer and we shall acknowledge him to be
our superior."

"If he cannot, then we must request that he be sent back to his
own country."

The King agreed, and ordered his nobles to join him in the
Hall of Audience.

There was soon a huge assembly in the great hall, and all the
cleverest men in the land were there. The Persian sage rose
from his seat at the King's command and made a gesture towards them, without saying anything at all. The clever ones of

11

Cairo were all confused and said, "O Sire, we cannot guess what this learned Persian means. Grant us a delay of six days that we may talk among ourselves and try to understand this thing."

The King allowed them six days in which to unravel the problem and they all went their separate ways.

In the coffee-houses and studies of the learned sheikhs the question was asked again and again: "What could the Persian sage mean? How could he be answered and sent back to his own country?" But though the beards wagged night and day there seemed to be no answer. Then one sheikh said, "Let us find a village lad who does not know anything about learning and ask him what this might mean. Perhaps in his ignorance he might stumble upon the answer, as we have seen that children sometimes do."

So one old Sheikh went out into the bazaars of Cairo, and lo, just outside the gates of Al Azhar, he came upon a lout straight from the fields who was selling some carrots and an egg. He caught him by the shoulder and said, "O my son, come with me, I wish to talk to you."

The poor peasant was very frightened, and his face went grey. He hid the egg and the bunch of carrots in his shirt, as he thought that the long-bearded old Sheikh was going to ask him to give them up, for he had no idea what to expect in the great city.

The Sheikh saw that the lad was frightened, so he tried to soothe him and asked, "What is your name, my good fellow?" To which the lout answered, "Abdulla, O great Sheikh," and fell silent, wondering if it were possible for him to make a break for it and run, for he felt awkward standing there talking to a long-beard of such wisdom and knowledge as this Sheikh of Al Azhar.

"Now, Abdulla," said the Sheikh, "I want you to come with me to a Persian gentleman who talks only by signs, and I want you to reply to him in the same way. For this Persian has challenged us here in Cairo to a contest, yet he will not speak, only make signs. Now, if you will do this and carry it out successfully, you shall be richer by several piastres." "Oh, sir, may you live for ever!" cried Abdulla. "I shall be most happy to oblige, for I am several piastres in debt and cannot sell my carrots today, or this egg, no matter how much I try."

"Capital fellow!" said the Sheikh. "Come with me and I shall let you meet all the other sheikhs and sages with whom the Persian has already disputed in sign language without success."

When the other sheikhs saw the village lout they almost collapsed with laughter, for he was a comical sight with his long, coarse face, patched shirt, bare feet and horny hands. However, they put a long cloak upon his back, a turban on his head, and fine leather slippers upon his feet. His bunch of carrots and the egg he would not allow to be taken from him, and he kept them hidden inside his shirt, close to his chest. Thus arrayed, Abdulla was led out to do battle with the Persian in the great Hall of Audience, with viziers and amirs in a large circle around the King.

The King sat on his marble throne, and said, "In the name of Allah the Merciful, let the discussion start."

The black slaves beat upon gongs, and the proceedings began.

The Persian rose from his cushion, bowed, and sat down again. And the peasant sat down, too, on a low divan, with no more concern than if he were in a cattle-pen.

Then the Persian arose from his cushion and pointed with one finger at the peasant, and Abdulla answered by pointing two fingers. The courtiers watched with bated breath.

The Persian put his hand up and kept it there for a few seconds. Whereupon the peasant placed his hand on the floor, deliberately.

The Persian took out a box, opened it, and pulled a hen out. He threw it to the peasant. Abdulla put his hand inside his shirt and took out his egg, which he threw to the Persian.

At this the Persian shook his head and said to all the wise ones present, "Lo, this sheikh of yours has answered my question and I am now one of his pupils."

Then the King was well pleased, and rewarded the simple Abdulla with a bagful of piastres, which would be enough to keep him in comfort for many moons. The courtiers went home as mystified as when they had arrived at the Hall of Audience in the first place.

Before he returned to his village, the Sheikh who had brought Abdulla into the Hall of Audience said, "You did well and valiantly, my dear young man, but do tell me, what did all those gestures mean which you and the Persian made during the argument?"

"Well, sir," said Abdulla, "this was how I understood it. I thought when the gentleman pointed his finger at me it meant that he was saying, 'If you don't keep your eye open, I shall poke my finger into it - so.' And then I replied by two fingers - which I meant to represent, 'I shall poke out your two eyes if you start anything.' Then when he lifted his hand up and kept it there for a few seconds, I thought that he was saying, 'If you overcome me I shall hang you from the roof.' When he made this gesture I became angry and replied by putting my hand on the floor, which I meant to mean, 'If you treat me like this I shall dash you to the ground and bash your brains out.' Then when he saw me getting the better of him he took that box containing the hen out of his pocket, and threw it to me in order to say that he was in the habit of eating the finest flesh of chickens. Whereupon I threw him the egg I had been carrying about with me in order to show him that I too was in the habit of eating good things, that is, boiled eggs and suchlike. As you know, he was then convinced of my logic and said he would become one of my pupils."

Now, the Persian was going home to Ispahan by the next caravan, so the Sheikh went to see him off and said, "O Knowledgeable Persian, do tell me how it was that our young friend was able to dispute with you when he knew not a word of your language. Tell me, what meaning did you take from his gestures?"

"Only the correct meanings, of course," answered the Persian. "Your young man was clever indeed. In all the countries to which I have gone in order to dispute I have never yet, until today, found one who could correctly answer my questions."

"Please tell me, in order that I may benefit," pleaded the other,

14

and the Persian told him:

"Know, O Sheikh, that when I raised my finger towards him the first time it was as if to say, 'There is no God but Allah the One!' Whereupon by raising his two fingers he gave me to understand that Allah was God but Mohammed was His Prophet. When I raised my hand aloft to the roof for a few seconds it was as if to say, 'Allah supports the heavens without pillars.' And he put his hand on the floor as much as to reply that Allah was God of the Earth as well as the sky. Then I threw the hen towards him to tell him that Allah causes the living to be produced from the dead. He replied by showing me the egg, which means that He also produces the dead from the living. Thus it was that I received the answers to my questions, which I have asked in every capital in Asia, and never got the correct replies until now, which has pleased me very much. What a great brain your friend must have indeed; Allah's blessings be upon him!"

So the Sheikh of Al Azhar went his way wondering at the strangeness of life, and how curious it was that two people, so different in mind as the Persian and the peasant, should be able to converse in gesture entirely to each other's satisfaction without meaning the same thing at all.

Why the Cock never got back to Paradise

ONCE UPON A TIME, before Allah made the Earth, the birds were created and lived in the Garden of Paradise.

There were large and small birds, each one beautifully coloured with wonderful plumage, and the one with the loudest voice was the cock.

Among the trees and flowers of the garden they flew, with plenty to eat and the clear water of many springs to quench their thirst in the golden, sunny days.

The fruits and berries were so delicious, and the company of the angels so divine, that the cock became dissatisfied with his easy life, and longed for some adventure.

So he said to the angel who looked after the welfare of the birds, "Shining One, where may I go to have some adventure, some meaning to my life, for I do nothing of importance here, where all is goodness and light?"

And the angel answered, "Patience, brave Cock, for Allah the Merciful, the Compassionate, has ordered your estate."

Then the cock preened his fine feathers, and crowed aloud with pride, and said to the other birds, "I am soon to be given an

17

important post, watch me, I am going to surprise you all!"

The other birds said, "Brother, what sort of news is this? Are you not satisfied with life as it is, here in the sunshine of the garden, among trees loaded with the choicest fruits?"

But the cock crowed even louder, and flew high in the air, and was all puffed up with pride. For in those days the cock could fly as high as the eagle.

Then the angel came to the cock, and said, "Allah, the Merciful, the Compassionate, has created the Earth below us, and put in it all manner of beings, human and animal. You, O Cock, are to go there and take the news of Allah's Greatness to all those creatures."

"Am I to be a Herald, then?" cried the cock. "A Bearer of Tidings beyond compare?"

"No, no," the angel said. "Just take a journey there and back, telling the men, animals and birds below that tomorrow is the First Dawn. You shall crow to them in your loudest voice to proclaim the Greatness of Allah the One. Then you must fly straight back here. This is the message I am commanded to give you."

So the cock flew down to the earth, and the first dawn was breaking. He called in his loudest voice to the newly created, saying, "O Men, Animals and Birds, Allah sends me to welcome you to the World, and to tell you that I, the Herald of Allah's day, the bird with the loudest voice in the Garden of Paradise, have been chosen among all others for this task."

Amazed, the people who heard him, and the animals and other birds, bowed to the ground and paid the cock tribute.

The cock flew high in the air and demonstrated his great skill in flying, and his heart swelled with pride.

When night came, he was so tired flying about and showing himself off that he fell asleep, and forgot all about flying straight back to the Garden of Allah.

Several days passed, with the cock waking everyone each dawn with his clarion call, and still he was treated with reverence.

Soon he began to think that he was the most important creature in the newly-created world, and strutted among the new humans, shaking his feathers, looking around him with arrogance.

Then the words of the angel came back to him, and he thought to himself, "I had better fly back to the garden now, and take no time about it, for I have a feeling that I may have stayed here upon the earth too long."

He gave a loud cry and gathered his legs up beneath him, and fluttered his wings, ready to soar up into the heavens once more.

But, though he tried again and again, there was no power in his wings. He merely flew up a few feet and then fell to the ground again.

Thus the great pride of the cock was his undoing, and his forgetfulness of Allah's word caused him to remain a prisoner on the earth. So, you will often see the cock flapping his wings against his breast, trying to gain his former speed, but he never can fly higher than the garden fence.

The Story of Hatim Tai

A LONG TIME AGO, in ancient Arabia, there lived a most generous and noble tribal ruler called Hatim Tai.

He was the chief of many tents, for in those days the tribes of Arabia wandered from pasture to pasture with their flocks, and several tribes claimed his protection. He had a great deal of land and wealth.

Now, as the tribesmen under Hatim Tai grew more and more numerous, the King of Arabia became jealous of his reputation as a great tribal overlord.

"How dare this Hatim Tai set himself up as a leader of men?" said the King. "Everyone speaks of him as if he were greater than myself! His kindness, his generosity, his fair-mindedness — he seems to be a paragon of all the virtues. I am tired of hearing about him. I think that his manner of getting my people to gather around him is a treasonable matter!"

"It is indeed, O King," said the Vizier, who was also a bit of a hypocrite. "Your Majesty is right, as always. Shall orders be given to have him beheaded?"

"No, no," said the King, "he shall die in battle. Tell the Chief

21

of the Army that we march on the tents of Hatim Tai as soon as we can get every soldier in the whole of my dominions together. We shall soon see who is mightier, Hatim Tai or I!"

Now, when preparations had been going on for some days and the troops were massing for a battle, news came to Hatim Tai.

"The King of All Arabia, being jealous of your power in the land, has declared war upon your tents, O Hatim Tai!" cried a tribesman, pulling at Hatim Tai's robe as he was sitting drinking a cup of coffee outside his tent one morning. "Arm the men of the tribes, and fight back!"

"If the King of Arabia hates me," said Hatim Tai, "then it is nothing to do with my tribesmen. Why should they have to lose their lives and cause their widows to weep, just because one man is envied by another? I will go and hide in the hills until the situation changes. The King will forget me, and perhaps some day I can return."

"We shall strike camp this very day," said the elders of the tribe, "and travel on to other pastures, for if Hatim Tai does not want us to fight we shall not do so."

Then, while the women and children packed up the cooking-pots and tent hangings, the men dismantled their tents. They drove the camels and flocks before them, into the desert, looking for a place to camp.

Hearing that Hatim Tai had fled, and his tribes scattered, the King of Arabia was very angry and said, "What a coward this famous, generous man must be! As soon as he hears that my army is ready to do battle he runs away like a desert rat. The people must see their leader for what he is worth, now he has shown what a weak man he is in reality."

"O Great King of Araby!" said the Vizier, "let me send soldiers far and wide to search for Hatim Tai, for his treason is still a punishable offence. Also, let a price be put on his head, for he is an enemy of Your Majesty, and deserves to die an ignoble death!"

"Excellent," said the King. "Let a proclamation be read in the *souks* and the *khans*, wherever people gather in numbers. A thousand pieces of gold to the man who brings him to justice!"

22

And all Hatim Tai's wealth was seized.

There were many in the land who knew where Hatim Tai was hidden, and no one betrayed him to the soldiers who were searching for him. To almost everyone Hatim Tai was a legend, and he remained free for a long time. Secretly, people sent him food and clothing in his mountain hiding-place, so he did not starve.

There lived in that deserted region an old man and his wife, who collected wood to make into charcoal. One day, they came near to where Hatim was also gathering some branches for his fire. He heard them speaking and hid behind a rock.

"If by the Mercy of Allah we could ever find Hatim Tai, would it not be wonderful, for then we could go to the King and get a thousand pieces of gold!" said the old woman, as she bent herself almost double to pick up a twig.

"Silence, wife, never say such a thing again, even if you live to be a hundred years old! How could we give Hatim Tai to the King? It would not be worth twenty thousand pieces of gold if we were to do such an evil thing. It is our *Kismet* to be charcoal burners and Allah will not forsake us if we walk in the right path."

Grumbling a little the old woman bent down again; and at that moment Hatim Tai came from behind the rock. "Allah has heard you today," said he, "I am Hatim Tai. Take me to the King, and you shall be richer by a thousand pieces of gold."

"Oh, no, generous Hatim," wept the old charcoal burner. "Never think this of us, for it was only a wicked impulse which Eblis the Evil One put into my poor wife's mind! Sell you to your enemy for gold? May Allah be my judge, I shall not be the cause of your death this way."

"Come, take me," said Hatim Tai, "if my life can benefit you and your poor wife, so that you could be secure for the rest of your days, and I shall be happy. What use am I to anyone up here, living in a cave like a hunted animal?"

But while the old man was protesting, a party of soldiers came up silently and listened to all that was said. They heard Hatim Tai, and saw who he was. Before he knew what was happening the soldiers seized him and took him away. The poor charcoal

23

burner and his wife followed them, not knowing what to say.

The King came out and saw the huge crowd of people in the courtyard and asked the Vizier: "What is happening? Why all this noise and hubbub?"

"Your Majesty," said the Vizier, "they have found the traitor, Hatim Tai, and have brought him to justice at last."

"Who found him?" asked the King, "and where?"

At this, all the soldiers began shouting and each said it was he, until the King raised his hand and silenced them. "You cannot all have a thousand pieces of gold," said he. "One only must have found him, and to that one I shall give the reward."

Hatim Tai spoke out and said, "O King of Arabia, the one who found me is that old charcoal burner. Give him the gold, for his need is greater than that of these soldiers who only brought me here."

"Your Majesty," cried the old man, "Listen, I beg you, to the truth. Hatim Tai himself came to my wife and myself and said we were to take him so that we could get the money. He heard my wife say, when we were collecting wood, that the thousand pieces of gold would keep us in plenty for the rest of our lives. While we were protesting, these soldiers came up and took Hatim Tai prisoner, because he was not looking out for them."

Listening to this story, the King of Arabia's heart was touched, and he saw that Hatim Tai was indeed as generous as legend had made him out to be. He was ashamed, and made a sign to the soldiers to release Hatim Tai's arms.

"Let him go free," he said, "and return him to the tents of his people, for it is proved beyond all doubt that Hatim Tai is the most noble man in the whole of our dominions."

Hatim Tai stood for a second before the King, and then gave thanks to Allah for His Mercy that day. The King ordered a thousand pieces of gold to be given to the old couple, and restored all Hatim Tai's wealth to him.

When the news reached the tribesmen that their chief was at liberty again, they came in great numbers and accompanied him to their new territory. And the King of Arabia allowed Hatim Tai and his people freedom for ever and ever.

The Three Brothers
and the Fairy

ONCE UPON A TIME there was a man who had three sons. He asked them what they would like to be, so that they could go out into the world with a chance of earning good money.

"I would like to become a champion marksman," said Abdul, the eldest. So his father agreed that he should be trained by the finest hunter in the land to use the bow and arrow.

The second son, Ahmad, said "I would like to become an astrologer, and learn the secrets of the heavens." He was sent to study under the wisest star-gazer in the kingdom.

When it came to the turn of the youngest son, he said "Father, I would like to become a carpenter." At this his father became most annoyed and said "A son of mine a common carpenter? Would you bring shame upon me, in my grey hairs?" But the young fellow, whose name was Mahmud, persisted, and finally the old man agreed.

When three years had come and gone, all three were trained in their chosen professions. Abdul was such a fine marksman with the bow that he could bring down a gazelle at twenty paces while galloping across the desert. Ahmad could read the signs and symbols of the stars by putting his spy-glass to his eye, and was offered a post at the Court of the King. The boy who had learned carpentry was declared by his master to be the best wood-worker he had ever known.

But they could not settle down in the town of their birth, for each longed to see the world and taste adventure before they died. So they went to their father, and each begged a purse of money that they might journey for a while before beginning their careers.

"Very well," said he, "here is the money. Go in peace and return when a year is past."

The three brothers dressed themselves in clothes suitable for travelling, and set out, on horseback, to find adventure.

The first night they were sitting beside their camp fire, talking happily together, when Ahmad looked up at the heavens with his spy-glass and said, "Brothers, there is a very strange and brilliant star shining over us at the moment. That means momentous events are about to occur."

No sooner were the words out of his mouth than there was a loud sizzling noise, and a beautiful fairy, dressed from head to foot in flame-coloured draperies, stepped out of the middle of the fire.

"Mortals," said the fairy, "my sister has been put under a spell, taken away by a wicked witch, and imprisoned in a tower. My powers, alas, cannot reach as far as the tower, but if you do as I say, you shall all three be rewarded."

They all agreed, and the fairy continued: "You must ride for one day from here, taking the direction to the south, until you come to the tower. You, Abdul, must shoot the arrow which will kill the witch. When she dies, my sister will be free."

"Are you sure she will die?" asked Abdul.

"I shall smear some of this magic ointment on the arrow," said the fairy, "and she will die instantly. When you have rescued my sister, I shall appear to you again." So saying, the fairy disappeared.

As the dawn was breaking, they kicked out the fire and mounted their horses, riding south all that day. As the sun was

26

setting they came to a tall white tower, set in the middle of a dismal desert. There was a strange silence, broken only by the frightened snorts of the horses as they pawed the ground.

The brothers decided to camp a little way from the tower, and when the moon was shining, Ahmad put his spy-glass to his eye and saw a beautiful fairy, dressed in silver draperies, looking out of a window at the top of the tower. The three brothers called loudly, "We have come to save you; wait, let the witch come to the window!" No sooner had the witch heard the noise of their shouts, than she bundled the fairy into a cupboard and came to the window.

"What do you want?" cried the witch. "Be off with you or I shall turn you into snakes!"

But no sooner were the words out of her mouth than Abdul's arrows pierced her heart, and she fell out of the tower window on to the ground. Her body was instantly turned into ashes as they watched, and blew away like dust.

"Now how are we to free the fairy?" asked Mahmud, but at that moment the beautiful creature flew down from the window, having escaped the instant the witch was dead.

"Thank you, good mortals, for saving me - how did you know I was a prisoner?" she asked.

"Your sister, the flame-fairy, appeared to us last night," said Abdul, "and she said that she would come again when you were free." As he spoke, the other fairy appeared in their midst, and the two sisters kissed with cries of joy.

"Mortals!" the fire-fairy told them, "you shall now receive your reward. Up in that tower the witch has hidden a lot of rich treasure. Look, there is a door hidden at the base. Open it and climb the secret stairs leading to the storehouse. Peace and blessings be upon you. If you ever need us, call upon us in the name of Suliman, Son of David, King of Magicians, whose slaves we are!" And the two fairies vanished.

In the bright moonlight, the brothers opened the hidden door to the secret staircase, and found the storehouse was stacked from floor to ceiling with jewels and golden ornaments, silks and robes fit for princes. They dressed themselves in the

27

grandest clothes they could find, and put jewelled harnesses on their horses as well. The whole treasure was too vast for them to carry away, so the brother who was a carpenter made them three small boxes, into which they put the finest gems and the most valuable jewellery.

No sooner had they done this than the enchanted tower vanished from sight. The three boxes they buried in the ground and covered them up before it was light. Then they lay down and fell fast asleep in their silken clothes, dreaming of a life of luxury.

While they slept a band of robbers crept upon them, and, thinking they were nobles, tied them hand and foot with ropes. In the morning, the three brothers woke to find that they were prisoners and the robbers were sharing out their clothes and money.

"Ho-ho, noble sirs," said the chief of the robbers, prodding them with his foot, "what a fine sight you are, tied together like hens in a market-place!" The robber chief was an ugly-looking man, with a patch over one eye, and a ragged red beard.

"Let us cut their throats!" shouted the robbers, and danced round, waving their knives.

"In the name of Suliman, Son of David, save us, flame-fairy!" cried Abdul, as he saw that he and his brothers were going to be murdered by the robber band. There was a sudden flash of light, and flames rose and crackled all around until the robbers were burned to ashes. Then the flame-fairy appeared and waved her hands over the brothers. Their bonds fell off as if by magic, and they stood up rather shakily to thank the fairy for her kind help.

"Let that teach you a lesson," said the fairy. "Never travel richly dressed like that, attracting the attention of robbers and brigands. The treasure which you have buried is safe; dig it up, load it into your horses' saddlebags, and ride from hence, otherwise you will get into more trouble. If you need me, call me, but I can only appear to you once more!"

Sadder and wiser, the brothers dug up the treasure they had in the boxes, put as much as they could safely carry in their saddlebags, and rode northwards to their home.

A few days later, after the brothers had eaten their midday meal, a terrible sandstorm blew up. Horses and men had to lie down huddled together, with their cloaks over their heads, trying to shelter from the stinging sand. The sky grew as black as night, and the wind howled with the voice of a thousand devils.

When everything was calm again, and the horses scrambled to their feet, the brothers found that they were hopelessly lost. They did not know which way to turn, and they were tormented by thirst.

"I would give all our treasure if only we were able to see the stars!" said Abdul.

"Well, let us call upon the fairy again," said Mahmud.

Then, together they called "In the name of Suliman, Son of David, King of Magicians, come to us, so that we can ask a favour for the last time."

In a moment the flame-fairy appeared before them.

"Where are we?" they cried. "Help us!"

She said cheerfully, "Half a mile's ride from here will bring you to a river in the valley below. There you can drink, and water your horses, and will find wood so that you can make a raft to take you to the other side. Wait on the other bank for the night, and then, with the aid of the stars, you may return home. Now, good-bye for ever." Then she vanished.

The brothers rode on for another half-mile, and sure enough, as the fairy had promised, a broad river flowed at the bottom of the valley. The brother who was a carpenter started to make a raft from the pieces of wood which were lying about. Soon they ferried their horses and themselves over to the other side. A whole flock of wild birds flew overhead, and Abdul fitted an arrow to his bow in a trice: one bird fell to the ground. They made a fire and cooked the bird, and waited for night, when Ahmad would be able to find the way by the stars.

"I want to see no more of the world," said Abdul. "I shall be quite happy to settle down now, with my share of the treasure, and teach others to shoot."

"Yes, I too will be happy to go home and spend my life as a carpenter," said Mahmud. "Now I can buy a shop and new tools, and be a credit to father."

Soon it was dark, and the stars came up, and Ahmad read the

29

direction they should take. They travelled all night and at dawn came within sight of the town of their birth.

"Praise be to Allah!", cried Abdul, "we shall never wander again for the rest of our days, brothers."

And they never did.

Poor Hasan
and the Magic Talisman

A LONG TIME AGO, there lived in Jeddah, on the shores of the Red Sea, a poor man called Hasan.

He made a living by boiling salt water in shallow pans, and then collected the salt which was left behind when all the water had evaporated. One sultry afternoon in July, the sun was hot, and his feet were scorched by the hard, burning sand.

Hasan scraped another pile of salt from the dish he was holding, and filled it again with seawater. Out on the sea he could see a ship approaching, manned by sixty black oarsmen. A man with a drum was beating out the time high on the poop deck.

He shaded his eyes and watched the ship coming nearer.

It was the Viceroy of Jeddah himself, arriving to collect his dues from the people of the port. In snow-white robes and head-cloth, the Viceroy stepped from the ship, his slaves and advisers following. Hasan knelt in respect as they proudly passed in their fluttering draperies.

The sixty black slaves, their bodies glistening in the sun, marched along, silver collars around their necks. A pair of cheetahs, trained for hunting, came next with their Nubian attendant.

Then two men with hawks on their wrists, which were for catching birds in flight for the Viceroy's sport. The chests for the tax-money which was to be collected were carried by fierce-looking men armed with daggers stuck in their belts.

Hasan watched the procession with open mouth. The proud Viceroy of the Caliph, the noble entourage, the haughty servants and mighty oarsmen, all filled him with admiration and awe.

"Oh, if only I were rich and powerful," he cried "How happy I would be! How is it that Allah should have made me poor and miserable and the Viceroy so rich and happy? If only I could exchange my piteous fate for that of the Viceroy of Jeddah, surely I would be the most contented man alive."

Now, at that moment, he found in the salt-pan a square of discoloured metal, which appeared to be engraved with some ancient letters of the alphabet. Rubbing the curious-looking object between his fingers as he spoke, Hasan continued, "If I could but change places with the Viceroy for even one day..." And at his words the sky suddenly became black. The sun was obscured, and Hasan felt himself swept up into the air, like a bird. For a space of time he whirled above the Earth, and a voice said in his ear: "You have in your hand a most powerful talisman, which has the magical property of granting each wish you utter while you have it in your possession. Therefore, be the Viceroy of Jeddah, as you desire!"

The sound of the tempest died away, and Hasan found himself sitting on a divan in the Viceroy's palace attended by slaves on every side.

The tax-gatherer was saying to him: "May Your Highness live for ever! The money which we have extracted from the people is in this chest, and the money donated by the nobles and dignitaries in the other. May it please Your Highness to watch while we count and weigh the gold, in order that the true figures may be assessed and taken to our sovereign lord the Caliph."

Hasan nodded, not daring to speak, in case he said the wrong thing.

He held his breath, while more money than he ever knew existed in the world was counted and weighed. It was poured

32

into money-bags and sealed with his own signet ring at the tax-gatherer's request.

No sooner was the money weighed and accounted for in a book, than the Chamberlain announced that the day's petitioners were about to come in for judgement of their claims.

This took several hours, as each case had to be reported in full. The final word was to be Hasan's, and every point was discussed. It was a wearisome business for Hasan, who had imagined that the life of a Viceroy would be one of luxury without labour. The Chamberlain had opened the proceedings for yet another petitioner, when Hasan said to himself: "By Providence, what a tedious matter this has turned out to be!"

He rubbed the strange talisman he had found in the salt-pan between his finger and thumb, and wondered if he should try another wish.

"In the name of our sovereign lord, the Caliph!" cried the Chamberlain, and Hasan said to himself: "If I were the Caliph, I am sure I'd be much happier than I am at this minute! By the power of this talisman, I wish I were the Caliph!"

No sooner were the words out of his mouth, than there came to his ears the sound of rushing winds, and the voice which had spoken to him before said, "Go, mortal, the wish of the moment is granted. Be the Caliph!"

Hasan opened his eyes to find that he was sitting on a carved marble throne in the middle of a huge Hall of Audience. Courtiers in rich brocades were grouped around him. Gigantic Negro slaves with unsheathed blades stood at the doors, the hafts of their swords set with diamonds and rubies. Three hundred emissaries of every nationality were standing round the walls, which were decorated with gold letters a foot high, describing the Attributes of Allah the One. Behind the throne, concealed by screens of the richest filigree silver, were the ladies of the court, discreetly silent.

Hasan looked down at his clothes, and saw that he was wearing a gold-embroidered tunic, and a suit of the finest chainmail. His boots were of glistening leather, ornamented with jingling spurs of gold Damascened work. Upon his right arm was tied a silver talisman, engraved with the Throne Verse from the Holy Koran. A page, also in chain-mail, was approaching the Caliph with a huge, double-edged sword on a cushion of green velvet.

"Lord of Islam!" said the page. "Here is the Sword of Right, take it in your right hand, and slay the Infidel for the blessed Cause!"

He held it before Hasan, with bended knee.

Hasan picked up the sword, and felt its weight. It was as much as he could do to lift it. What was going to happen? Why had he wished to be the Caliph at that moment?

There was a great deal of clamour in the courtyard outside, and the people in the Hall of Audience looked apprehensive as there came knocking at the huge doors. The Captain of the Guard opened the doors, and the General of the Caliph's forces burst in. He flung himself down before the throne.

"The Mongols of Genghis Khan are almost at the gates," he gasped. "Lead us to battle, Caliph of Islam, or let us waken in Paradise!"

The people rushed forward as the Caliph rose from the throne. There were cheers and cries of joy when he fixed the sword into its scabbard at his waist.

But though to the people Hasan looked a figure of power and strength, his heart was afraid. He quaked in his chain-mail armour. In his left hand he still held the ancient talisman of blackened metal, so he rubbed it, saying under his breath: "I am likely to lose my life very soon if I go to lead the troops against the hordes of Genghis Khan, so let me please be a humble man again, with my salt-pan on the shore at Jeddah!"

No sooner had he said these words, than the sound of rushing wind was in his ears, and he closed his eyes.

He felt himself swept over land and sea to the hot humid air of his native country. When he opened his eyes, it was the same scene he had known so well. The sun was blazing down upon the sea, and there was a sharp tang of salt on his lips.

"Allah be praised!" cried Hasan, kneeling down and kissing

the ground. "I shall never be dissatisfied with my lot again. The Viceroy and the Caliph have their own troubles. Let me accept my own *Kismet*."

Somewhere during his last journey the magic talisman he had held in his fingers had been lost, but Hasan was not sorry. He returned to his old life grateful that he could do so, and lived contentedly until the end of his days.

The Date Merchant
and the Generous Man

ONCE UPON A TIME there was a man called Abdul Majid
who was a date merchant.

One day, on his way to Mosul to see his broker about the
latest shipment of dates, he fell from his horse and injured his
leg.

Seeing a large house near by, with fine gardens all around it
and a huge brass-studded door, he knocked and waited.

Soon there was the sound of bolts being drawn, and a very
tall, handsome man, wearing an embroidered cap, a silk gown
and yellow morocco leather slippers, opened the door.

"Peace be upon you, traveller," he said grandly, bowing with a
majestic air. "What do you need?"

"Peace be upon you too, brother," said Abdul Majid. "I have
fallen from my horse and injured my leg. May I wait here until it
is better?"

"By all means," said the other at once. He led Abdul Majid to
a divan. His horse was stabled, and bedded for the night. Slave
boys massaged his leg and dressed it with fresh linen bandages,
his hands were washed with scented water, and a meal of the

37

finest boiled mutton cooked with spices was brought by a Circassian girl.

He knew no more until morning. Then he was awakened by the same finely-dressed man, whom he took to be the master of the house, and delicious fruits were spread before him.

"This is wonderfully generous of you," said Abdul Majid, as he struggled to his feet.

"It is nothing," said the man, helping Abdul Majid up, and he dressed him in fresh garments as lovingly as if he had been a brother.

Next day Abdul Majid's leg was so much better that he was able to mount quite easily, and he rode round in the grounds to get his horse ready for the road.

Standing at the door, watching him, was a thin, grey-haired man in patched clothes, with a white beard and broken sandals.

"What a poor old man," thought Abdul Majid, as the other's greeting came to his ears.

Then the splendidly-dressed man came towards Abdul Majid and handed him a bag of provisions for the journey.

"Thank you very much indeed," said Abdul Majid, as he rode off, "may Allah reward you!"

The tall, handsome man bowed gravely, putting his hand to his heart.

Time passed, and it was about six months later that business took the date merchant to that place again.

This time he met a pedlar on the road as he passed the great house, and said to him: "Last time I was here I injured my leg, and the greatest hospitality was shown to me by the owner of that estate."

"Alas, Allah gives and Allah takes away!" said the pedlar. "The master of that house has died. He is a loss to us all because of his generosity and kindness, and he always did good in secret, without ever taking the credit for it himself."

"How very unfortunate! May his soul rest in Paradise," said Abdul Majid. "I will go at once to the house and offer my condolences to the family."

He rode up to the gate as before, and knocked on the brass-studded door.

It was opened after a few minutes, and Abdul Majid was just about to offer his sympathy, when he stood back in amazement.

For the person who had opened the door was the same tall, handsome man dressed in fine clothes and yellow morocco leather slippers.

"How wonderful to find you alive!" said Abdul Majid, "I heard that you had died!"

"No," replied the man, "it was not I who died, but my dear master, the most generous man in the world of Islam. He denied himself luxuries so that he could give to others. May his memory be green for ever!"

"Your master? But - I thought you were the owner of this house and grounds," said Abdul Majid.

"When you came before," said the servant "do you remember a frail, white-bearded old gentleman in a patched robe? Well, that was my master."

The Jinn's Son and the
Three Magic Threads

A LONG TIME AGO there was a female Jinn who assumed the form of a beautiful girl.

She was sitting in a tree, singing to herself, when a king chanced to ride past.

"What sort of bird is this which sings like a maiden?" said the King, and stopping his horse, he looked up into the branches.

He saw a girl as fair as the moon and begged her to come down, saying, "I am alone and travelling to the city. Will you not join me while I sit and eat my meal in the shade of this tree?"

And so, veiling herself, the female Jinn came down, and ate with the King. When the time came for him to go, he said, "I have been looking through the length and breadth of my land for a wife. If I go home without one, my people will laugh at me, because I have not been able to make up my mind."

"I cannot marry you," she said, "for I am a Jinn, and you who are Believers are expressly forbidden to marry us, for we are creatures of fire, and Allah created you out of flesh."

"No one will ever know," said the King. "Come with me, and

41

you shall be my queen. Everything you ask for shall be yours, whatever it may be."

"Very well," she said, "I will marry you, but you must never ask me what I am doing. I must have my own way in everything, remember. If you ever ask me, I shall disappear, and you will not see me again."

The King promised, and the beautiful Jinn got up behind him, and away they went.

They arrived at the capital city of that land and there was much rejoicing when the King announced his marriage. There was a great feast at the palace, and money was distributed to the poor. Huge torches blazed in the courtyard far into the night, and musicians played the merriest tunes. After the celebrations were over, everything soon returned to normal, and the King became preoccupied with affairs of state. He began to give less and less time to his new wife. Although she had everything which she desired, yet she became lonely for those of her own kind. One day she went out into the garden, and climbed into a tree. She sat on one of the branches, singing to herself.

But the Grand Vizier saw her from a window and went to the King, saying:

"Oh, Most Excellent Majesty, the Queen has just climbed the pomegranate tree in the garden. Surely Her Majesty will fall if she goes any higher?"

The King looked out of the window and shouted: "My dear, come down from that tree. What are you doing?"

As soon as he spoke he remembered that he should not have asked her what she was doing. The King came into the garden, to look for her and apologise, but it was too late. She had completely disappeared. He tore his clothes and grieved for her, but she never came back.

After a year, the people clamoured for a new queen, and this time the bride was the daughter of a neighbouring prince.

The Jinn returned to her own people, and spoke no more of the time when she had been married to a human. In time a son was born to her, and grew up tall and handsome, exactly like his father.

When the boy, whom she named Shahbush, was eighteen, his mother said to him:

"You must leave us now, for we are Jinn, and you are the son of a human king. Go to your father's kingdom, and take these three pieces of thread. If you ever have need of help, tie a knot in a piece of thread, and blow on it. I will rescue you from whatever threatens you."

Then she gave him instructions as to how he could reach his father's kingdom, and he set off.

When he arrived at the capital city and announced who he was, everyone who saw him marvelled at his likeness to the King. There was a great crowd around him as he knocked at the palace door.

The doorkeeper stared hard when he saw the young man and said:

"Is Your Excellency a relative of our Sovereign Lord the King?"

"He is our Prince!" shouted the people. "Take him to His Majesty!"

The Grand Vizier came and took Shahbush to the King, and his father was overjoyed to see him. His second wife had only produced three daughters. He had a throne placed beside him in the Audience Chamber and announced to the court: "This is the son of my beautiful first wife, whom you remember disappeared. He is the one who shall rule after me."

The second wife grew green with jealousy, and planned to have the young Prince killed at the very earliest opportunity.

She bided her time until the King and the Prince went hunting with their retainers, and sent for her slave, Musa the Ethiopian.

"See to it that the Prince does not return," she said, "and you shall be well rewarded."

"To hear is to obey," replied the slave.

Musa the Ethiopian followed the royal party at a distance, and when the Prince was separated from the others, he pushed Shahbush into a deep pit. The young man lay stunned and unconscious for hours.

Musa the Ethiopian, thinking that his victim was dead, triumphantly returned to the palace, and the Queen gave him a bag of gold.

When they found the Prince was missing, the King and his courtiers looked everywhere, but could not find him.

"Alas," said the King, "what can have happened? He came just when I needed him so much, and now he has suddenly vanished."

"His mother disappeared too, did she not?" said the Queen cunningly. "Think no more about him, my lord, for it is obvious that he is just as strange as she was."

But the King still had hope that his son would be found.

As soon as Shahbush came to his senses, he realised that he could not get out of the pit. He heard the voices of the hunt servants calling him in the distance, but the pit was so cleverly concealed that they did not find it. He remembered the threads which his mother had given him, and took one of them out of his pocket. He tied a knot in it, blew on the knot, and called his mother's name.

In less time than it takes to tell, Shahbush saw a golden ladder from the pit to the ground above. He quickly climbed up and as soon as he reached firm ground, the ladder vanished. He met some of the searchers, and in great excitement they took him back to the palace.

The King gave thanks to Allah for his son's delivery, but the Queen's face grew pale with anger. She sent for Musa the Ethiopian and said: "You told me you had killed the Prince. How is it that he is back safe and sound?"

"A thousand apologies!" cried Musa. "Let me try once more."

"If you do not succeed this time, your head shall roll!" said the Queen.

The Ethiopian waited until the Prince was asleep, and then he piled a lot of brushwood in front of the bedroom door. He lit the brushwood, and when the smoke was so thick and black that it would have suffocated ten men, the wicked slave opened the door. The smoke poured in, and no one knew until the whole of the Prince's quarters were burning. Finding himself trapped behind a wall of fire, Shahbush just had time to take one of the

44

magic threads from under his pillow, and knot it. He blew on the knot and called his mother's name.

In less time than it takes to tell, the flames died, the smoke cleared away, and he was safe once more.

At the failure of this plan, the Queen became more angry than ever. She said to Musa the Ethiopian, "Try again, and if you do not succeed, may Allah have mercy upon you!"

Musa thought of another idea, and disguised himself as an old woman.

When Shahbush was out riding, he stopped at the sight of a poor tattered creature, weeping into her kerchief as if her heart would break. "What is it, grandmother?" said he, and dismounted.

"Oh, oh, oh, my husband, my husband!" wailed the crone. "Taken away by a lion, up there in the mountains!"

Now, in truth, there was a lion which had become a man-eater, and Musa thought if the Prince could be lured to its cave, that would be the end of him.

"I will see what I can do," said Shahbush, giving her the reins of his horse to hold. "Stay here until I come back. I may be able to save your husband." Then, taking out his hunting knife, he began to climb up towards the lion's cave.

The lion's roars came loudly and fiercely to Shahbush's ears; but he climbed steadily on, getting nearer and nearer to the man-eater.

As soon as he heard the lion, Musa the Ethiopian's nerve failed, and he mounted the Prince's horse and galloped away.

The lion came out with a rush, and Shahbush stabbed him with the hunting knife. There was a growling noise from the lion's throat, and then no more. The man-eater was dead.

Shahbush looked round for the old woman's husband but there was no sign of any living thing in the cave.

"Poor man, the lion must have eaten him," thought Shahbush to himself, and he climbed down to where he had left the old woman and his horse. As soon as he saw that both were gone, he took out the last piece of thread which his mother had given him. He knotted it, and blew, calling his mother's name.

As soon as he had done so, the Ethiopian fell from the horse,

45

hampered by the female attire he was wearing, and broke his neck. The horse flew like the wind and returned to its master. Soon Shahbush was back at the palace, and related his adventure to the King. He also realised when he saw her face that the Queen was behind the plots to kill him, and the King banished her to a tall tower where she could do no more mischief. So Shahbush did not need his mother's protection again.

When Shahbush became King after his father's death he ruled the country for many years, and there was peace and happiness for all the days of his reign.

Small Abdul, the Ogress
and the Caliph's Daughter

ONCE UPON A TIME there lived a man called Big Abdul, who took his wife and child with him on a pilgrimage to Mecca.

When they were nearly there, the pilgrim caravan was attacked by brigands. The woman and her son were carried off to the brigands' lair.

"You shall do the cooking for us," said the brigand chief.

"I will do anything you ask," she answered, "as long as you do not harm my son."

"Harm that dwarf?" laughed the brigand. "He is no larger than a doll. Why should we trouble about him?"

Time went by, and Small Abdul was growing up. His mother was always hoping that one day she and the boy would be able to escape from the brigands, but they firmly locked the cave door when they went off on their raids. Inside the cave there were sacks of treasure, chests of gold and jewels, and bales of rich stuffs.

One night, the brigands came back with a string of camels, which they tied up outside the cave. "Woman!" they shouted, "bring the food, we have had a tiring day!"

While Small Abdul's mother was giving the rogues their meal, he crept out of the cave. The very best camel he could see was at the end of the string, so he untied it. While the men were eating and drinking in the cave he whispered to his mother: "Come, we will escape tonight, when they are all asleep." No sooner had the brigand chief and his men eaten, than they sprawled on the ground and went to sleep. Now was the time for Small Abdul to bring the camel to the cave entrance. He made it kneel, and helped his mother into the saddle. Then he got up behind her, and they were away like the wind. It was a moonlit night, and the camel went across the desert as fast as it could go.

Now the camel, which was a *mehari* or racing camel, belonged to the sheikh of a certain tribe. It carried Small Abdul and his mother swiftly back to its master's encampment, for its young one was there. In the early dawn they arrived, sore and weary, at the sheikh's tent. The camel knelt, and they got off. When the young camel was being fed by its mother, the sheikh thanked Small Abdul for returning his favourite animal. "Small Abdul," said the sheikh, "you must stay here with us, and be brought up with my own sons. Your mother will be a sister to my womenfolk, and you shall never want for the rest of your lives."

"Thank you very much for your kindness," said Small Abdul, "but my mother and I have to go on and find our way home. My mother wants to know if my father ever returned home, if he is alive or dead."

"Take one of my camels, then," said the sheikh, "and continue your journey after you have rested three days in the encampment. I can never repay you for what you have done."

So for the traditional three days they had the best that the sheikh's people could offer. A feast was prepared, and Small Abdul was given a sheep's eye as a sign of great favour. When the time came for them to go, the sheikh gave them his blessing, and a bag of provisions for the journey home.

All the people came from their tents to wave good-bye, and the sheikh told them the direction to take.

At long last Small Abdul saw the white houses of a town on

48

the side of a hill.

"Allah be praised!" cried his mother. "We have arrived back safe at last!"

Five years had passed since the poor woman had set off with her husband for Mecca. She scarcely dared hope that her husband had got home safely from the looted caravan. If he had it was possible he had taken another wife, or maybe four, according to the Muslim law.

As soon as they rode into the town, Small Abdul made the camel kneel. Then he and his mother made their way to their old home.

There was Big Abdul sitting on the floor, eating his midday meal.

"Husband! Do you know me?" said the woman. "Small Abdul and I have had such good fortune. We escaped from the brigands, had many adventures, and here we are, safe and sound."

"By Allah!" Big Abdul jumped to his feet. "What a miracle to see you alive! I never thought I would set eyes on you again. How wonderful are the ways of Allah the Compassionate."

"Look," said Small Abdul, "here is a bag of jewels which I brought from the brigands' cave, and we have a camel which a sheikh gave us. We shall not be penniless but will have plenty when we sell the jewels."

"My dear son," said Big Abdul, "our troubles are over."

When some time passed, the Caliph's daughter Akila was carried off by an ogress. She was abducted one day when she was playing in the garden and imprisoned in a room in the ogress's gigantic castle. The Caliph's soldiers attacked the castle, and fired their arrows over the walls into the courtyard. But the arrows merely glanced off the ogress's thick skin, and they could hear her laughing after each attack.

Then the ogress began to throw boulders down on them, and they had to run and hide, or they would have been crushed.

After a while a proclamation was read out to the people by an official from the Caliph's court.

"Whoever can kill the ogress and save the Lady Akila shall be given as much gold as he wants, whether he is high or low,

Believer or Infidel!" shouted the official.

"Small Abdul," said his mother, "you go and save the Caliph's daughter. I know you can do it."

So Small Abdul waited until it was dark, and climbed up the hill to the castle. He threw a rope over one of the gates, and dropped into the courtyard. All around him were bones of all shapes and sizes, shining in the darkness.

He went up the staircase and looked into all the rooms until he found the ogress. She was lying asleep, snoring very loudly, on a huge pile of furs. There was a sword hanging on the wall, and Small Abdul took it down. As soon as he was armed he gave a shout and the ogress woke with a start.

"Who dares to rouse me from my sleep?" she snarled.

She jumped from her bed and the floor shook. Small Abdul hid behind a cupboard as she blundered round the room looking for him. "I can smell Man!" she said, angrily, getting down on her hands and knees. At once Small Abdul cut off her head with his sword; and that was the end of the ogress.

Where could the Caliph's daughter be? Small Abdul opened all the doors and searched the castle from top to bottom. In the very last room he found the Lady Akila hanging up by her beautiful long hair. He untied her, and helped her down the stairs into the courtyard. Then, standing on Small Abdul's broad shoulders, she unbolted the big door. Outside, hidden in the darkness, were the Caliph's soldiers, waiting a chance to rush into the castle.

"The ogress is dead," said Small Abdul, "and the Lady Akila is safe." So they all cheered him and the Caliph's daughter, and carried them both back to the palace.

The Caliph was so delighted that his daughter was safe that he rewarded Small Abdul with a robe of honour, and said, "Even though you are so small, you have the heart of a lion! Come to the palace tomorrow, and a feast will be held in your honour, when you shall be given all the gold you will need for the rest of your life."

And the Caliph was as good as his word. The feast lasted for seven days and seven nights, and Small Abdul received from the

Treasury a hundred camel-loads of gold. He built a fine house for himself and his parents, and lived in luxury for many years.

Yunus and the
Well of Sweetness

ONCE UPON A TIME there lived a man called Yunus, who wanted to get married. He had often seen a pretty girl at the window of his neighbour's house, and wondered if she were of marriageable age.

He went to his neighbour, and said: "Brother, have you any objection to me as a son-in-law? I think you have a daughter who would suit me."

The neighbour answered: "Yes, indeed I have one girl left who really should be married now. But there is one snag."

"And what is that?" asked Yunus.

"Well, you see, she has got such a very bad temper that I hate to inflict her upon anyone, least of all such a good friend as yourself," said the other. "The only thing which must be done before she marries is almost impossible, I'm afraid. No one would go to all that trouble for my little Fatima, I'm sure."

"Tell me about it, please," said Yunus, "and if it is in my power, I will do it."

"I have been told," said the girl's father, "that three drops of water from the Well of Sweetness will be enough to cure any woman's bad temper."

"Let me go, then," said Yunus. "Where is the Well to be found?"

"The old woman who begs on the steps of the mosque knows," said the neighbour. "It has to be brought back in a tiny bottle, which holds three drops. But my dear Yunus, do not put yourself to so much trouble!"

"Think nothing of it," replied Yunus cheerfully, "I shall set off today." He bought a small bottle in the market, and went off to the old woman who was seated on the mosque steps with a begging bowl in her hands.

"Where is the Well of Sweetness?" asked Yunus, dropping a coin into the bowl.

"Seven days to the West, and seven days to the East, there you will find the river. Cross that, and you will come to the country where a Giant lives. Ask him, he will tell you what you want to know," she said.

Yunus travelled on and at last arrived at the river. The ferryman rowed him across, and Yunus asked him, "Where does the Giant live?"

"In that direction," the ferryman told him. "He has a cave in those mountains. But be polite when you speak to him, or he will hit you with his great club."

It was a long, weary walk, and when he arrived at the foot of the mountains, Yunus lay down and went to sleep. When he woke, he felt very warm and comfortable, and thought at first he must be in his own bed at home. But when he opened his eyes, he saw that he was lying in the palm of a gigantic hand.

"Hah-hah, little mortal, so you have come to visit me, have you?" said the Giant. "Who are you, and what do you want?"

"Most noble Giant," said Yunus, politely, "peace be upon you! I have come to ask you where I may find the Well of Sweetness. I only want three drops to take back to the girl I wish to marry, because she has a very bad temper."

"If you had not replied so courteously," said the Giant, "I would have crushed you like a fly! However, since I do not get many visitors who address me respectfully, I will tell you.

"Here, inside my cave, is a secret passage guarded by a three-headed dragon. Go along the passage, and when you see the dragon, say 'By leave of Suliman, Son of David (upon whom be

54

peace!), let me pass!' and the dragon will let you through to the Well."

The Giant then put Yunus down on the ground, and he entered the cave with beating heart. Sure enough, as he proceeded down the passage which the Giant showed him, there was a three-headed dragon, breathing fire and lashing a long green tail. "By leave of Suliman, Son of David (upon whom be peace!), let me pass!" said Yunus, and the dragon let him continue without doing him any harm.

After a long time there was a shaft of light ahead, and Yunus saw a beautiful fairy pulling up a bucket of water from a deep well.

"Peace be upon you!" said he, and the enchanted creature replied in a sweet voice, "Peace to you, mortal; come, I will fill your bottle for you." She did so, and handed it back to Yunus. He was so delighted, he kissed the fairy's hand in gratitude, but as he did, she disappeared.

Now he had to go back the way he had come, and it seemed twice as difficult as it had been before. The sharp stones cut his feet, and his hands were bruised as he felt his way in the gloomy rock-hewn passage.

At last he reached the fire-breathing dragon, but as soon as its six blazing eyes looked in his direction he said the magical sentence, and it allowed him to go past.

He got to the Giant's cave once more, and showed him the tiny bottle of water.

"Hah-hah, little mortal," said the Giant, "you have got what you wanted. Now you must work for me for a year and a day, and then you may go home."

So Yunus served the Giant for a year and a day, cutting grass for his goats, which were milked every day, and cooking the Giant's evening meal in a big pot. He washed the dishes, hung the huge shirts out on the bushes to dry, and kept the fire alight. When a year and a day had gone, the Giant was so pleased with him that he gave him a bag of gold, and allowed him to go home with the best of goodwill.

Yunus's neighbour came out of his house and said, "Oh, my

dear friend, I am so pleased to see you. Why have you been so long away? Did you get the water from the Well of Sweetness? We were afraid that something had happened to you."

So Yunus told him all that had occurred, and handed over the bottle containing the three drops of magic water.

Then he went home to his mother's house, and dressed himself in his best clothes, ready for the wedding. The Kadi came to perform the ceremony, and they went together to the neighbour's house.

After the contract had been signed, the bride appeared, veiled and jewelled, and Yunus felt himself to be the happiest man in the world. The bride's father gave the signal for the feast to begin, and everyone ate and drank to their heart's content.

That night Yunus took off his wife's veil, and found her to be as beautiful as anyone could wish. Her voice, when she spoke, was as sweet and soft as the cooing of a dove.

"Ah, dear wife," said Yunus, "what wonders there are in the world, Allah be praised! If I had not gone to get that water from the Well of Sweetness, I doubt if I would be as happy as I am to hear your voice tonight."

"Whatever do you mean, husband?" she asked. "My voice has always been like this."

"But your father told me that you were so bad tempered that only three drops of water from the Well of Sweetness would cure you," said he.

At that the girl threw back her head and laughed. Yunus demanded to know why she was making such fun of him, and shook her until she stopped.

"It was not I who had the bad temper," she said, "but my dear mother! My father was tormented by her spiteful tongue, and her rages. He was told by a wise man that a complete change would come over her if only she could have three drops of the magical water on her tongue. So, he decided that anyone who asked for me in marriage should go for the water so that my mother would be cured and my father saved from an early grave!"

Then Yunus laughed too, and was grateful that at least he

56

would now have a good-tempered mother-in-law. His new wife and he were so happy together that they never had a cross word for the whole of their lives.

The Merchant's Daughter
and the Golden Ring

ONCE UPON A TIME there lived in the city of Samarkand a rich merchant, who had two daughters. One he loved very dearly because she resembled her beautiful dead mother, but the other, the youngest, he did not like because she was not pretty.

Now, when the girls were of marriageable age, the merchant looked around for suitors for them. The beautiful girl, whose name was Ayesha, was married first, because her father gave a large dowry away with her. But the youngest daughter, whose name was Noora, had no portion and so no young men came to court her. After her sister left home, her father married again, and Noora became her stepmother's slave.

"Bring me this, and that. Go to the market, buy some sewing thread. Hurry, hurry, be quick about it!" cried her stepmother from morning until night.

Noora became very sad, and used to cry herself to sleep thinking of the days when her own mother was alive and all was happiness in the house.

One night, unable to sleep, she went outside into the garden and knelt down under the rose bush where her mother used to sit, and said: "Oh, rose bush, rose bush, let me water you with my tears. If only I were a child again, playing with your blossoms!"

59

And the rose bush answered: "Do not give yourself over to grief, dear mistress. Life was not made for sorrow."

"But how can I be otherwise?" said Noora. "I am my step-mother's slave and no one will marry me, for I have no dowry."

"Pick one of my rose buds," said the rose bush, "and you will find something inside which will help you."

Noora picked the biggest rose bud which she could see and opened it. Inside there was a small golden ring, with a strange design on it. She slipped it on to her finger. It fitted perfectly.

"What a wonderful rose bush you must be!" cried Noora. "How does it happen that there is a ring in one of your buds?"

"I am an enchanted rose bush," was the reply, "and this ring which you have just found is a magic ring, and belongs to Suliman, Son of David, King of Magicians. Because you have come to me in your need, I have helped you. With this ring you may be able to escape, for it grants a certain number of wishes."

"What shall I ask?" enquired the girl.

"Whatever you like," said the rose bush. "Say, 'In the name of Suliman, Son of David (upon whom be peace!), I wish for such and such...' "

Noora repeated: "In the name of Suliman, Son of David (upon whom be peace!), I wish that I were in a little house of my own, and had my own personal maid!"

No sooner had she said these words than there was a rushing sound as of a great wind, and Noora felt herself being carried through the air by invisible hands. She closed her eyes in fear, and held her breath. When she opened her eyes, she found herself in a room, lit by oil lamps hung from the ceiling and full of beautiful furniture and ornaments. She went through a carved wooden doorway and saw another room, where a table was set for a meal, and she seated herself upon a divan to get her breath back. At that moment a slave girl as brown as a date entered, and placed a dish of delicious food upon the table.

"Where am I?" asked Noora faintly.

"You are in your own little house, mistress," said the slave girl, "and I am your personal maid." And she began to serve the meal.

As if in a dream, Noora ate and drank, and then the slave brought rosewater for her hands, and burned sweet incense in the room.

Rising from the table, Noora found that there was a bed chamber which was stocked with everything necessary, and a cupboard full of fine clothes.

"What a wonderful happening," thought Noora, and went to sleep full of happiness.

In the morning she said to the magic ring, "In the name of Suliman, Son of David (upon whom be peace!), may I be given a purse of gold pieces so that I may go to the market." And within a few moments, there was a purse of gold in her hand.

Noora changed her much-worn garments for new clothes, and attended by her little maid, went out to the market to make her purchases.

Now, in her new clothes and veil no one recognised her, and even when she saw her stepmother buying fruit, Noora was able to pass her without being seen.

Meanwhile, at the rich merchant's house it was understood that the master's ugly daughter had run away, and no one even troubled to search for her.

Each day Noora went shopping and bought everything she required, returning to her own little house full of joy at her good fortune. One day, the slave girl went with the bed linen to the public wash house and Noora was left alone in the house. There was a knock at the door, and Noora peered through the lattice. Outside there was a tall young traveller.

"Greetings, my dear," said he, thinking she was the maidservant. "Will you tell me which is the house of the doctor in this street, for I am a stranger and have cut my hand badly." He held it up, and Noora could see the blood seeping through the rough bandage.

"Why, the doctor lives in the next house, but he is away from home. You must come in here and I will attend to it myself," said Noora, opening the door.

61

She pulled her veil over her face, and seating the young man upon some cushions she brought water and ointments for his wound.

"You are extremely kind," said the traveller. "I shall not forget this act; when I come to Samarkand again I will bring you a present."

Noora bent her head over her task, and said: "This will help to heal your hand quickly; you must use some more ointment from this pot in two days' time." And she put the small container into his other hand.

As she did so, her maid returned, and Noora, after asking her to bring tea, was able to disappear into her inner room. When the teapot arrived, Noora, still wearing her veil, returned to pour out tea for herself and the young man.

"You have been so very kind," said the traveller. "I shall go on my journey asking Allah to shower blessings upon you. Pray forgive my intrusion into your home."

"No intrusion, I assure you," said Noora. "Although I live alone here and have visitors but seldom, I should be happy if you would call upon me in order that I might satisfy myself that your hand was indeed better."

The traveller rose, thanked her again, and left.

"Mistress, what a handsome young man!" cried the slave. "He would make a good husband for you, if he is not married! He must be a person of good family for look, he has a fine horse with beautiful trappings, and he sits upon the saddle with dignity and pride."

"Hush, do not say these things," said Noora. "He was looking for the doctor's house, and was only pleased I could attend to his wound." And she sighed as she removed her veil, for she knew she was ugly and no young man would look upon her long without dismay.

Next day, when they went to the market, Noora was choosing some grapes from a stall, when a woman who was standing next to her saw the gold ring upon her finger glinting in the sun. Now this woman was a thief, and when Noora left the market she followed her, trying to get a chance to steal the ring. In a crowd of people looking at pots hanging outside the coppersmith's shop, Noora felt someone brush past her. She thought nothing of it until she returned home, and went to wash her hands. The magic ring of King Suliman was gone!

The thief, meanwhile, had concealed the ring in her mouth. Noora ran back the way she had gone, looking on the ground for the ring but there was no sign of it anywhere. She went home and began to cry.

"Mistress," said the slave girl, who of course was a fairy. "A female thief has taken your ring. I know this by the power invested in me by King Suliman, Son of David (upon whom be peace!), whose creature I am. Leave this to me. I shall find it."

She hurried out into the street. Noora looked out of the window and saw her disappear round the corner. "Whatever shall I do if I do not get it back?" Noora said to herself. "I will starve, for I cannot return to my father's house to be bullied by my stepmother."

Now, the slave girl ran on until she came to the market, and she looked about until she saw the female thief (who was well-known for her pilfering) sitting on the ground near a beadsellers stall. The woman was awaiting an opportunity, when the beadseller might turn his head away, to help herself to some small item. The slave girl, who had a pinch of pepper tied up in a knot in the corner of her handkerchief, untied it, and threw the pepper into the female thief's face. The woman sneezed, and the ring which she had concealed in her mouth shot on to the ground. The slave girl pounced upon it and ran away as fast as her feet would carry her.

She took it to Noora and placed it upon her mistress's finger. Noora was so delighted she immediately wished for a pair of fine gold earrings for the slave girl as a reward.

A week passed, and Noora began to feel that her life was empty. She had no friends, nothing to do, and plenty of everything. She began to think of the young man whose hand she had bandaged, and wondered what had become of him. Would he visit her again as he had said he would?

Just then there was a knock upon the door of her little house, and Noora looked down into the courtyard. It was the handsome young traveller himself, with a green birdcage in his hand. "Oh, how can I ever show my face to him, ugly as I am?" cried Noora, as the maid went to answer the door. "I must wish for a face which is pleasing, so that I may let him look on me with happiness."

So, twisting the ring upon her finger she said, "In the name of Suliman, Son of David (upon whom be peace!), make me beautiful!" No sooner were the words out of her mouth, than there was a noise like a clap of thunder, and a voice said in her ear, "Why cannot you be content with your own face as it is at this moment? If you ask for beauty then this is the last wish the ring can grant, and the ring and its power will vanish!"

Noora could feel the ring upon her finger grow hot, until it almost burnt her.

"Yes, yes," she cried. "Let me have beauty, and I will willingly give up the magic ring."

"So be it," said the voice, and Noora ran to her mirror. The face which looked back at her was just as she had always dreamed she would like to be. Her eyes were large and bright, her mouth small, her skin white. She smiled, and she saw her teeth were as perfect as pearls.

She turned round just as the slave girl entered with the traveller. When he saw Noora he fell in love with her at once.

"Peace be upon you, beautiful lady!" said the visitor. "I bring you a rare bird of the Orient which sings exquisitely."

He held out the green cage. Inside was a bird with golden feathers and a scarlet crest. Noora veiled herself and signed to the young man to sit upon the divan. The bird in the cage began to sing divinely.

"Thank you, sir," she said politely. "It is most kind of you to remember my humble help. It was nothing," she continued, "I am only glad that I happened to be here when you came."

The maidservant brought in a pot of tea, and Noora seated herself at the table, filling two cups with amber-coloured liquid.

"Dear lady," said the young man, "I have thought of no one but your lovely self since I left here, and could not wait until I could present myself to you again."

"Why, sir," said Noora, modestly, "I am glad that you came, but I did what anyone would have done..."

"If you are not a princess already, I would like to make you one!" cried the young man. "For I am the son of a king, who has spent a year looking for a bride both beautiful and kind. Now I have found you, will you do me the honour to become my wife?"

Noora agreed, and the prince took her away to his own country. Which was just as well, because the ring which had granted her wishes vanished from her finger, but they both lived happily ever afterwards. As for the little house in Samarkand and the slave girl who was as brown as a date, they both returned to the dominions of Suliman, Son of David, King of Magicians (upon whom be peace!).

The Princess
and the Dervish

ONCE UPON A TIME there lived a king who had a beautiful daughter called Leyla. From her earliest days she had been her father's favourite, for though he had three sons she was his only daughter.

Now, she was as happy as a bird, until the day that her father said to her, "My child, soon you shall be wed, for I have sent invitations to all the princes of the world, so that you may choose a suitor." At that moment, the Princess, who had been standing beside her father's throne, fell forward in a faint.

With cries of alarm, the ladies of the court clustered round and carried their mistress into the harem, where they laid her on a divan. The royal doctor was summoned, and he prescribed the burning of peacocks' feathers under the Princess's nose, and a pearl a day to be swallowed at midday. But the Princess Leyla never moved; her eyes were fast closed, and her pulse almost too faint to be felt.

For seven days and seven nights they watched over the unconscious girl, but she showed no sign of life. The King was seriously alarmed, and the three Princes, her brothers, rode to all parts of the kingdom to try and find a cure. On the eighth day, an ancient man in tattered robe and dusty sandals came to the palace.

"I can find out what ails the Princess," he said. Immediately he was taken to the King.

"If you can make my daughter waken, everything you desire is yours!" vowed the monarch.

The dervish smiled. "Take me to her," he murmured.

Then, beside the divan where the unconscious Princess lay, he knelt. He took the slim hand in his and placed his fingers upon her pulse. "Cairo," he pronounced. The pulse of the Princess showed no sign of quickening. "Damascus," he said. "Beirut", then "Jeddah". There was no reaction. Then the dervish whispered into the Princess's ear "Samarkand". At that moment he felt the pulse of the Princess Leyla leap under his fingers. "Lo," said he to the King, "bid the scribe write 'Samarkand'."

Once more the sage bent to the shell-like ear of the Princess and whispered "Silk. Ivory. Brass. Copper. Diamonds. Rubies. Pearls." At that the pulse of the Princess suddenly quickened. "Your Majesty," murmured the dervish, "we progress, there is a pearl-merchant in the city of Samarkand ... write down 'Pearl-Merchant', scribe."

"What are you saying, Dervish?" cried the King. "How can these riddles help us, in Allah's name? Will my daughter ever regain her sanity, or lie here for ever like one dispossessed of her wits?"

"Patience, O King," said the old man, "and all will be known. This is the only way to cure your daughter." Then to the Princess he said, "Short, Fat, Bald, Rich." The Princess slumbered on, her breast rising and falling with the breath of a child. "Tall, Dark, Handsome." The Princess stirred and her eye-lashes fluttered. Her pulse began to race. "Ahhh ..." the old man spoke. "Scribe, write 'In Samarkand there is a tall, dark and handsome pearl-merchant'..."

"What is his name?" roared the King. "If he has harmed my daughter in any way I shall have his head!"

The dervish raised a hand. "Peace, O King, I will just try and find out his name..." He began to murmur into the Princess's ear again "Mahmud, Omar, Ibrahim, Issak, Yunus, Muhamed, Abdul, Tahir, Talib, Ahmad...." At the last name the pulse of the

68

Princess gave another leap, and she opened her eyes.

"His name is Ahmad," said the dervish, releasing the Princess's hand.

"What do you mean?" the King demanded. "Who is this - this fellow, and what does he mean to my daughter?"

"You had better ask her yourself," said the dervish quietly, "look, she is awake at last." And sure enough, the Princess was stretching her arms above her head and smiling at all around her as if she had awoken from a refreshing sleep.

The King was so delighted to see her alive and well once more that he cried out, "O my daughter, tell me who this young man is and what he is to you. For this venerable dervish has discovered your secret."

"Dear father," said the Princess, "Ahmad the Pearl-Merchant was one of the suppliers of the Court jewels when my elder brother was married last year, and my mother the Queen said that I was to be decked in the finest pearls in the world for the occasion. Ahmad came with his merchandise and I fell in love with him. I had hoped when he went back to Samarkand that I would be able to explain about him and beg you to allow us to be wed. I was just about to tell you when you started to say that you were going to send invitations to all the princes of the world so that I could choose one as a husband. But my heart was given to Ahmad the Pearl-Merchant, and he loves me. If I cannot marry him I shall die. I know I shall!"

"In Allah's name!" cried the King, frowning. "This is nonsense; you must forget all about the young pearl-merchant of Samarkand. Such a husband is not for a Princess of my House. My daughter must become, in time, a Queen!"

"No, no. Please let me marry Ahmad," wept the poor girl.

"Enough," her father spoke sternly. Then, turning to the dervish: "Good sir, tell me, I beg you - what is your price for bringing my daughter back from her trance? Speak, and whatever it may be shall be yours."

"Anything I ask?" repeated the old man, smiling a gentle smile.

"Yes, anything it is in my power to grant. Also, you must stay for the wedding feast, when my daughter is married to a suitable prince."

"Then, give the Princess her wish," said the dervish, and looked long and hard into the eyes of the King. "I ask this as my reward, for I will take no other payment."

Then the King relented, and sent a messenger to Samarkand to tell the young man the news.

So the Princess Leyla married her pearl-merchant and Allah sent them many sons.

The Dream
Of Alnaschar

ONCE UPON A TIME there lived a certain barber.

Now, this man had five brothers, four of whom were hardworking like himself, but the fifth, named Alnaschar, was a dreamer.

One day, the barber received a visit from Alnaschar, who said to him: "Brother, my master died yesterday, and today, after he was buried, his wife turned me out of doors, saying she had no use for my services. Lend me, I beg you, a small sum of money, so that I can buy a few items of glass in the market."

"Glass?" asked the barber. "Why glass?"

"Because I will buy some beautiful pieces, take them and sell them to a rich man, like the Grand Vizier, for instance, and make my fortune."

"Stop dreaming, Alnaschar," said the barber, handing his brother three pieces of gold. "Go, buy the merchandise, and sell it for the best you can get. Forget about making a fortune, with Allah's help you may just be able to earn an ordinary living if you start properly."

Alnaschar thanked him, and set off for the market of the Glassblowers. He spent some time making a selection, and at last chose some very fine pieces. When he had bought them, he asked the glass-merchant to put them carefully in a basket with some straw. This the man agreed to do, and soon Alnaschar was on his way home with his precious load.

"What a fine selection of glass I have here," he said to himself gleefully. "Perfume flasks, goblets, sweet-dishes fit for the grandest in the land." Forgetting his brother's words, he began to see in his imagination great scenes of splendour, sumptuous feasts at which his glassware was being used by nobles and courtiers.

He sat down beside the road, placing the heavy basket with its delicate contents carefully beside him.

"At the house of the Grand Vizier," thought Alnaschar, "I will be treated as an equal, because of the beauty of my fine glass. The Vizier's daughter, a lady of unsurpassed fairness, will see me through the lattice as I show one fabulous item after another to her father. She will say to her nurse, 'I shall marry Alnaschar the Glass-Seller or no other! Go, tell my respected parent my wishes, let him draw up the marriage contract at once!' " Alnaschar nodded off to sleep in the heat of the noon-day sun. His head dropped. In his dream he saw the daughter of the Grand Vizier coming to him, veiled and mysterious, hung with jewels, breathing the scents of Araby. His arms outflung, Alnaschar rose in his sleep, and knocked over the basket of glass. The sound of breaking glass woke him, for a camel had kicked it in passing. Alas, not one piece of the merchandise remained whole!

The Pedlar's Son
and the Geni of the Well

ONCE UPON A TIME there lived a pedlar, called Wali. He used to go on long journeys to sell his wares, taking a camel laden with provisions so that he could travel for long distances at a time.

One day he got so far from civilisation that he completely lost his sense of direction, and let the camel find its own way across a desert tract. Just as night came, the camel trotted into a small oasis, and Wali saw that there was a well under the palms. The moon rose, the stars glittered in the sky, and the camel drank from the bucket.

"What a beautiful place this is," said Wali aloud. "I wonder what its name is? What a haven of peace and contentment!"

No sooner were the words out of his mouth, than a huge head appeared from the water and a loud voice said, "This is my oasis, and I am the Geni of the Well. How dare you drink my water without asking permission, mortal man?"

Wali was terrified and said, "I beg your pardon, mighty Geni. I shall leave at once."

"No, not so," said the Geni, angrily. "You have defiled my well and I must kill you for this. You shall never leave this oasis alive."

73

"Have mercy upon me," said the pedlar. "Ask me for anything, and I will give it to you, if it is in my power."

"Very well then, grant this request. You must give me whatever your wife hands you upon your return home," said the Geni.

"Agreed," said the pedlar, "I promise. But how am I to get it to you? I may not be able to find this well again. It is far away from all human habitation."

"That is how I prefer it," said the Geni. "Do not worry, I shall be able to come to your house, and when I materialise there, which I can, due to the power invested in me by the King of the Jinn, Suliman, Son of David (upon whom be peace!), you must make good your promise." So saying, the Geni disappeared into the depths of the well again.

Wali fell asleep, and in the morning thought he must have dreamed the whole episode. For there was no sign of the Geni when the dawn came. All was peaceful and quiet. Wali rode off with a light heart, and his camel took him quickly over the desert sand until they reached home.

When Wali reached his wife's apartment, she said, "A thousand welcomes, husband. See what Allah has sent us in your absence." And she placed in his arms, a newly-born child. "Your son, the answer to all our prayers."

"Oh, wife," said Wali, "I wish that you had not given him to me in this way, for a wicked Geni made me promise to let him have whatever you handed to me on my arrival home." For Wali suddenly remembered the Geni's words, and knew it had been no dream, but reality.

"No, no, husband, we can never give him up," cried his wife. "Put a magic talisman around his neck, and that will avert all evil."

So Wali went to a wise old man, who wrote a Koranic verse upon a piece of silver, which was sewn into a small leather bag. The pedlar's wife put it round her son's neck, and the child grew well and strong. When he was ten years old, the boy, whose name was Ramadan (because he was born during the month of Fasting) was playing in the street with his friends, when the

74

Geni of the Well appeared suddenly in their midst.

"Pedlar's son," called the Geni, "come with me and live in my beautiful oasis, far away from these dusty streets and crowded houses."

The other children scattered and ran away.

"No," said Ramadan, "I cannot leave my father and mother," and he went home as fast as he could to tell his parents what had happened. The Geni, seeing the magic talisman around the boy's neck, was not able to carry him off by force, and disappeared with a snarl of rage.

When the pedlar and his wife heard the story, they became afraid for the boy's safety, and went to the wise old man to ask advice.

"As long as your son wears the talisman, he is safe," said the sage, "but if he loses it, the Geni will be able to take him."

So they impressed upon Ramadan the necessity for wearing the leather bag around his neck at all times, and he never left it off for an instant.

Years passed, and the pedlar and his wife had forgotten all about the Geni. On his seventeenth birthday Ramadan enlisted in the army of the King, and went away to fight in the wars.

One night, the enemy attacked the camp where he was sleeping, and in the confusion and alarm Ramadan ran hither and thither, fighting as bravely as he could. But he was outnumbered, as there were two of the biggest and fiercest of the enemy soldiers attacking him at the same time. Just as he was about to be killed the Geni appeared and plucked him from the very midst of the fight. The enemy fled when they saw the gigantic monster in their midst.

"Hah-hah!" said the Geni, "I had to save you, because your father promised you to me, and I am protecting my own property. One day I shall have you!"

"Thank you, Geni," said Ramadan, "a thousand thanks for your help."

"Quick," said the Geni, "take off your talisman and come with me."

At that moment there was a flash of lightning and a burst of flame, and Suliman, Son of David (on whom be peace!), King of the Jinn, appeared in a glittering jewelled robe.

"Stop threatening this young man," said Suliman, in a voice of thunder. "Listen to my words."

"I hear and obey, master," said the Geni, throwing himself upon the ground.

"Geni of the Well," said Suliman, "according to our rules, you were an Evil Geni, condemned to live in the well for your past misdeeds. Now, for saving the life of this mortal, you are pardoned, and you may join the ranks of the Good Jinn, who stand on the right hand side of my throne. You are liberated, and have no more need to inhabit the well." Then to Ramadan he said, "Go, human being, and live in peace."

As suddenly as he had appeared, the dazzling King of the Jinn vanished, taking the Geni with him.

Ramadan returned to his companions, and they arrived home at last with much rejoicing. And many a night Ramadan sat beside the fire and told his parents and friends the story of the Geni, who nearly carried him away to some secret lair in the Mountains of Kaf, where the Geni dwell.

The Tailor's Apprentice
with too much Imagination

ONCE UPON A TIME there lived in Cairo a young tailor's apprentice. He used to daydream as he sewed away, sitting cross-legged in his master's shop. In his imagination he was always a prince, or a nobleman, wearing the finest clothes. In reality his name was Daud, and he was an orphan.

One day, a servant brought a splendid cloak into the tailor's shop. It belonged to a rich merchant, and needed shortening a few inches.

"Have it ready by tomorrow," said the servant, "I shall be back for it before midday."

"It shall be ready, if my shop has to stay open all night," promised the tailor. He set to work, and had nearly finished it, when it grew dark. "If I do not go back for my evening meal," said he, "my wife will give me such a scolding that I shall never hear the end of it." He gave the cloak to Daud, and told him to continue sewing the lining until he returned.

After he had gone, Daud, working steadily away, had soon finished the alteration. The merchant's cloak was of a fine brown wool, and Daud put it around his shoulders to see if the hang was right. It fitted him perfectly. Stepping back to see himself in the mirror, Daud thought he looked every inch a gentleman. He put on a pair of the tailor's red morocco leather slippers, tied a white linen around his head, and then he felt he could have passed as a nobleman. "I could go into the world and make my fortune," he said to himself. "No one would ever know that I was Daud the tailor's apprentice."

Rummaging under the counter, where he slept when the shop was closed, he took out his life's savings and tucked the small bag into his belt.

Before his master returned, Daud ran into the street, and soon put a mile or two between him and the shop without being noticed

He went into a coffee-shop, and ordered a meal. It was very late, and the café was crowded. A few minutes later a young man of his own age joined him at the table. They soon got talking, and after a while the newcomer began to tell Daud all about himself.

"I have just come to the town for the first time in my life," said the young man. "I was brought up by an aunt and uncle in the country. When I was born, my father had a dream which upset him very much. In this dream an angel appeared to him, telling him that unless I were sent away to a place of safety, I would die. At this time my parents were living in Alexandria, and disease and famine were in the city. So, I was sent to my mother's sister, who had a child of my age at the time. My own mother died and my father moved to Cairo, but was not able to send for me until this month, when I celebrated my eighteenth birthday."

"What a curious story," said Daud, intrigued. "What is your name, friend, and how are you to meet your father now you have arrived?"

"My name is Jabir," said the other, "and I am to meet my father at this very coffee-shop, and this is the hour when he is supposed to come. Do you see this dagger? I must hold it in my hand so that he will know me, and I am to say, in response to his greeting: 'I am he whom Allah has preserved!' and he will reply, 'Praises be to the Lord of the Worlds!'"

He handed Daud a beautiful dagger made of the finest

Damascened steel, with a scabbard decorated with turquoises.

As Daud held the dagger in his hands, he imagined himself as the returned son and found himself repeating the phrase the other had just told him. Jabir excused himself for a few moments to go and see about his horse, leaving Daud with the dagger while he was gone.

No sooner had he disappeared than a tall, noble-looking old man came up to Daud, and greeted him. "Peace be upon you," he said.

"I am he whom Allah has preserved," said Daud, as if in a dream.

"Praises be to the Lord of the Worlds!" cried the old man and embraced Daud affectionately. "My dear son! After so many years! I would have known you anywhere!" Daud was about to speak, but the other silenced him. "Come with me," said the old man. "Your path and mine will now be the same, and I shall tell you what plans I have for you."

Jabir had not yet returned, so Daud, tempted by the opportunity, went with the old man to a large house on the outskirts of Cairo. Here the rooms were luxurious and beautiful, and Daud felt at last his dreams had come true. He thought of the old man as his father, and had completely forgotten the unfortunate Jabir, whose place he had taken.

The deluded apprentice, imagining himself as the old man's rightful heir, sat down on the divan and looked about him as the evening meal was brought in.

An old servant, called Hamid, was pouring the drinking water. Hamid could not believe that this was his master's son, and felt sure that something was wrong. He whispered into the old man's ear: "Are you sure this is your true son?"

And the master answered: "Of course, how else could he have had the dagger and known the phrase to say to me?"

Suddenly, there was a loud knocking at the outside door, and in a few moments Jabir came in, shouting: "There he is, the rascal who stole my birthright!"

"No, no" said Daud. "Father, believe me, I never saw this man before in my life!"

79

"Which is which?" cried the old man, "I cannot tell who is telling the truth."

All unnoticed, the servant Hamid crept up behind his master and slit his robe with a knife. At that, the tailor's apprentice, seeing the tear, took a needle and thread from his pocket and started to sew it up.

Then Hamid pointed to Daud, and said, "Look this must be the runaway tailor's apprentice! The police have been looking for him the whole evening. Not an hour ago they came to this door; they were making enquiries at every house."

Daud ran to the door, but Hamid was too quick for him. He caught hold of the wretched apprentice and tied his hands with a piece of string.

"Jabir, my son," said the old man, "then you are the one, not he," and he embraced his rightful son at last. "I forgive you," he told Daud. "Go your way."

The unfortunate Daud was taken back to the tailor's shop, where the cloak he had stolen was returned. The police wanted to take Daud away, but because of his master's pleading, he was released.

"This ridiculous apprentice of mine," said the tailor, "suffers from a vivid imagination, and I can quite understand that he was tempted to take the cloak and impersonate a young man of quality. As he is an orphan, however, I will forgive him, and take him back into my service, as he is not a bad hand with the needle!"

So Daud learned his lesson, and tried to make amends.

In time he lived down the story of his escapade, and became a good tailor like his master. He inherited the shop, and never let his imagination get the better of him for the rest of his days.

The Prince, the Teacher
and the Eagle

ONCE UPON A TIME there lived a Queen, whose husband died when their son was only five years old. She was appointed as regent, until the boy was eighteen and able to rule.

The Queen's one fault was that she loved her son Hasan too much, and allowed him to do anything he wanted. So, though she was a good monarch in every way, her son became more and more wilful as he grew up.

One day she sent for the Grand Vizier, and said to him:

"Tell me frankly what I can do with my son. He is impudent, high-spirited, and altogether too difficult to control. What can be done to correct his faults now before it is too late?"

And the Vizier answered:

"Put the Prince under the care of a teacher, so that he may learn wisdom."

"Where is there a teacher who can help my son?" said the Queen.

"There is an old wise man at the moment in this city, on his way to Al Azhar, the university of Islam. If I go to him and tell him of the Prince's need for his tuition, perhaps he will come."

"Bring him here at once, if you can," said the Queen.

So the Vizier went off and returned with the teacher, who took

81

the Prince into his care.

Every day the old man and the boy would sit studying and reading.

The teacher told him of the wonders of the world, the wisdom of the Holy Koran, and the exact science of algebra.

Every week the Queen would send for the teacher and say to him, "How is my son progressing?"

And the teacher would simply shake his head and go away.

One day the Queen said, "How is my son progressing now, teacher?"

"He has not yet learned that a prince should be humble, that a king is the servant of his people, and that there is no power save that of Allah alone."

"What can we do?" said the Queen.

"Let me take him on a journey, Your Majesty," said the teacher. "If we could be nearer to nature perhaps I could help to change his ways."

The Queen agreed and the two set out wearing simple clothes such as travelling mendicants wear.

Now, at the end of the first day's journey, while they sat making coffee beside a small fire, two birds came as if from nowhere. They settled on the old man's knapsack, and began to twitter.

"I learned the language of the birds years ago," said the teacher. "But I regret now that I did."

"Why is that?" asked the Prince.

The teacher would not at first tell the boy what he meant, and the birds flew away. Hasan pestered him to answer, and at last he did so.

"The first bird was saying that in the time when you are king, there will be much joy for the birds who eat fruit. Gardens and orchards will be neglected, and birds will be able to feast there in peace. There will be no one to drive them away because the people will have gone from the land; they will not remain under such an unpopular king."

"What did the other bird say?" asked Hasan.

"The second bird said that there would be so many locusts to eat, he would be happy too. There would not be enough people left to burn fires in the fields and smoke the locusts out when they came," was the answer.

Next day, they reached an oasis where there were two camels drinking. When the travellers filled their water bottles, each camel started grumbling and grunting, as camels do, and the old man smiled to hear them.

"What are the camels saying?" asked the Prince.

At first the teacher would not tell, but Hasan persisted, and at last got him to speak.

"They are complaining that in the time when you are king, there will be so many people here, watering their animals and getting ready to leave the country to seek a livelihood elsewhere, that they will scarcely be able to get a drink," said the teacher.

For some days the old man and the Prince travelled on, and when they next came to a halt it was at the bottom of a high mountain.

On top of a rocky ledge there was a nest of young eagles with the mother bird perched beside it.

As they approached, they could hear the female eagle screaming to her chicks, and the old man translated:

"She is telling her young ones that when they are fully grown and you are on the throne, they must hunt for fat lambs in the kingdom next to yours, for the ones here will be thin and scraggy. Lizards and snakes will sun themselves among the ruins of your capital city, and the great mosque will be empty on Fridays when you are king. Unless..."

He stopped, but Hasan said: "Please, do tell me what the eagle says."

"She says that if you mend your ways now and improve day by day, then your name will be loved, and your kingdom will be happy and well-populated."

The Prince did not speak, but the teacher could see that he was thinking about what had happened. "Shall we go back to the palace now and continue with our studies?" he asked. Hasan nodded his head.

They went back the way they had come, and the teacher was pleased to see that his pupil was becoming more thoughtful and polite day by day. When they returned home again Hasan seemed at last to be able to understand what his lessons were about and now he really tried to learn.

The old man went to the Queen and said:

"Soon I shall be able to go, for the Prince is now getting ready to become a king. He will be a good one because he knows now that before one can rule others, one must be able to rule oneself."

The Queen was delighted, and offered the teacher a post at the court. But he said: "No, I must continue on my way, for I have a lot of work yet to do."

When the time came for Hasan to be king, he remembered the things his teacher had taught him, and ruled wisely and well until the end of his life.

The Princess and the
Crocodile-Hunters

ONCE UPON A TIME there lived a King and Queen who had seven daughters and one son. One day the King sent his son away with a tutor to learn the wisdom of the world. They went to a holy man's cave deep within a mountain, and after three years the young prince had learned how to name all the stars in the sky, how to add all the numbers in the world and how to speak the language of the birds.

"We must return to the palace, Your Highness," said the tutor, "for the holy man has taught us all he knows."

So they thanked the ancient man and set off for home. No sooner had they arrived back than the Queen burst into tears and cried, "Alas, alack, a wicked magician has been here in your absence, my son, and has turned your father the King into stone. Look, there he sits upon the throne, as cold as marble. What shall we do?" and she began to lament and tear her hair.

"Hush, Mother," said the Prince, "I will look up in the sky and see what the stars say."

He waited until night fell, and looked up into the sky. All the stars twinkled as bright as diamonds, and they said to him, "Go as far as the River of the Crocodiles, and the King of the Crocodiles will tell you what to do."

So the Prince went to bed and slept until the cocks crew, then he got up and dressed himself as a beggar. He said goodbye to his mother and seven sisters, and said, "Take these seven white stones and look at them often. If they turn black, send a servant to help me, for I am going to find the King of the Crocodiles, and ask him how to help my poor father." And he put the stones on a big brass plate.

Eveyone wept when he went away but they soon forgot to look at the stones every day. The six eldest sisters danced and sang and played with their golden toys, and they never thought about their brother, Prince Mahmud, who had gone on such a perilous journey to try and help their father. Only the youngest sister, Princess Soraya, carefully looked at the stones each night before she went to bed, and one Friday night she saw they were all black. She ran into her sisters' rooms, but they were asleep and she could not wake them. So she put on a tattered hooded cloak belonging to her old nurse, and set off to find her lost brother.

The moon was full, and she walked on until she came to an old tree, with huge branches reaching up into the sky. She looked up into the tree and said to the Spirit of the Tree, "Good Spirit, tell me if my brother has passed this way."

And the Tree Spirit answered, "Where was your brother going, little Patched-Cloak?"

"He was going to find the River of the Crocodiles," the Princess replied.

"Ah, yes, of course; he passed this way about a week ago. You must curl up in my lower branches and sleep until the sun rises, then you should take the left road and ask again when you get to the next big tree."

Soraya thanked the Tree Spirit and went to sleep gratefully in the shelter of the great gnarled trunk.

In the morning, as the sun rose, she ate a little of the bread she had in her pocket, and a few dried figs, and set off along the road. When midday came she had walked a long way and, sure enough, there was another large tree at the crossroads.

Soraya was very thirsty by now, so she was delighted when

she saw that there were delicious juicy fruits among the leaves. "Spirit of the Fruit Tree!" she cried, "may I quench my thirst with one of your fruits?"

And the Spirit of the Fruit Tree answered, "Certainly, my child, have as much as you wish. It is my pleasure to help travellers on their way."

"Did my brother pass this way, seven days ago?" asked the Princess. "He was going to try and find the River of the Crocodiles."

"Yes he did, I remember," the Tree Spirit answered. "If you want to go the same way as he did, walk on until you come to a gateway, and ask the Spirit of the Gate which direction your brother has taken."

When the Princess got to the gateway, she was so tired she could scarcely keep her eyes open. She whispered to the Spirit of the Gate, "Has my brother passed this way? The Fruit Tree Spirit told me to ask you."

"Your brother, the Prince, went through the Gate about six days ago," replied the Spirit of the Gate, "and if you walk on for another two hours you will come to the River of the Crocodiles."

After a rest in the shade, Soraya set off again. At last she came to the banks of a tremendous river, where crocodiles swam in the muddy water. She bent down and said to one crocodile lying in the sun like a big brown log, "Can you tell me how to find my brother, who came to visit the King of the Crocodiles about a week ago? Something may have happened to him, for the magic stones which he left have all turned black, and I fear that he may be in peril. The Tree Spirits told me which way to come."

"Our King holds court on an island not far from here," replied the crocodile, swimming up to the bank, "so if you get on my back I shall take you to His Majesty."

Soraya jumped on to the crocodile's back, and soon she was stepping ashore on a green island where tall coconut trees grew and crocodiles of all shapes and sizes lay in the sun. The largest and oldest crocodile of them all was sitting on a huge wooden platform right in the middle of the island.

87

When Soraya began her story, he said, "Ah! I know who you are!" showing all his gleaming teeth, "you must be the sister of the poor young Prince who was here a week ago."

"Yes, Your Majesty," replied Soraya. "The magic white stones which my brother left behind turned black, so I knew that something had happened to him. Oh, tell me, please, where is my brother now?"

"My child," said the Crocodile King, "he came to me to find out about the secret word which would turn the King, your father, back into his proper shape. I told him the word and no sooner had I done so than my great enemy, the King of the Crocodile-Hunters, came with a fleet of war-canoes against us here on the island. After much fighting, we managed to drive the Crocodile-Hunters away; but alas, they took your brother prisoner, and I fear he must be in great danger in their land."

"Where is that?" wept the Princess, "and how can I find him?"

"Wait until it is dark," replied the King of the Crocodiles, "and I shall lend you a log-raft. You can paddle this over to yonder bank, where the Crocodile-Hunters live. Then you must intercede for your brother, if he is in their hands, by using your prettiest words and much flattery. The King of the Crocodile-Hunters is very prone to flattery, and will do anything for you if you tell him he is handsome and elegant, although he is one of the ugliest creatures in the whole world!"

The King gave her a coconut and she drank its milk gratefully. Then she rested under the coconut trees until night fell, and when it was time, the crocodiles brought her a log-raft, on to which she climbed rather uncertainly.

The King of the Crocodiles reassured her. "The raft will not overturn, for it is made of the stoutest balsa wood, and you can easily paddle to the Land of the Crocodile-Hunters if you try."

And it was as he said, for Soraya was carried by the current so that she only needed to guide the raft with the paddle, and soon the raft came to a halt on some soft sand. She walked towards a brightly-lit building, where tall guards with spears barred her way.

"What do you want, Tattered-Cloak?" shouted one. "This is

the palace of the King of the Crocodile-Hunters, so go back whence you came. Our master does not have ragged vagabonds at Court!"

"Please," pleaded the Princess, "allow me to see your noble and excellent King, for I have a favour to ask him. One that concerns my brother, a prince; I am a person of noble blood like His Majesty the King, and I beg an audience."

The guards refused to let her pass, but the King's son was leaning out of the window and saw Soraya in the courtyard, and he fell in love with her despite her tattered appearance.

"Ho, guards," he called. "Allow the beggar girl to come in." And he said to himself: "If she were washed and dressed in fine clothes she would indeed be a splendid creature!"

Soraya was taken to the women's quarters, and bathed and dressed in a gown of finely-woven silk, with golden slippers on her feet; she looked as beautiful as the moon on her fourteenth night.

The King of the Crocodile-Hunters was sitting on his ivory throne, with his son at his right hand, when the Princess was led into the audience chamber.

"Why, this is a most fitting match!" said the King, for his son had told him that he would marry this fair stranger or no other. "Tell me, Lady, who is your father, and why are you so far from your own country?"

"O Most Excellent and Exalted Monarch!" began Soraya, "may the Sun in shame hide his vision from your brilliance, for you outshine everything in this world!"

"Well spoken!" smiled the vain King. "Tell me more; leave out no details, for I could listen to any amount of your fine phrases!" and he beckoned to the Princess to sit upon a silken cushion at his left hand.

"I have come upon an errand of mercy, your Magnificent Majesty!" said Soraya, prostrating herself before him and clasping his knees. "My poor brother, the light of my father's eyes, came to the Land of the Crocodiles to learn a magic word from the ruler of these regions, for my unhappy father has been turned into stone by a wicked magician. Now, in a fight with the

89

crocodiles, my brother, the Prince, was taken prisoner, and I believe is held captive by Your Majesty. Please, in your wisdom and enlightenment release the unhappy man, so that he shall return with me to our country, for unless we return, my mother the Queen will surely die of grief, and our dominions will be plunged into eternal sorrow."

Hearing these words, the King of the Crocodile-Hunter raised the weeping girl to her feet and said, "Of course I shall release your brother, for your words have moved me to the most profound pity."

"A thousand blessings upon your name and the members of your noble house!" replied the Princess, veiling herself as she saw the gaze of the Prince of the Crocodile-Hunters upon her. "I shall never cease to pray for Your Majesty's life all the rest of my days!"

"Bring the prisoner here," commanded the King, "for I have just learned from this sweet lady that he is none other than a prince who was on an errand of mercy. We cannot justly keep him here any longer, so prepare a fleet Arab steed with fine trappings and let him go home. What a mercy it was that we rescued the unfortunate fellow from those dreadful crocodiles!"

Within a few minutes, Soraya and her brother were reunited and clasped in each other's arms.

The Prince of the Crocodile-Hunters stepped forward and said, "Father, I claim this lady as my bride; she shall stay with us here for ever, and never leave these shores again!"

At these words the Princess felt her heart sink, for she did not love the Prince of the Crocodile-Hunters. She would have run from the hall, but her brother whispered in her ear, "Make no sign yet, but tomorrow we can escape together from this place. I have a plan."

So she allowed herself to be led away to the women's apartments, after giving her thanks to the King for her brother's safe delivery.

Next day, after the midday meal, Soraya was sitting at her window, looking out over the garden, when a little bird flew on to her hand and said, "Princess, your brother tells me to say that he will meet you in the garden at the fountain at midnight, for he has a way of escape from here."

"Why, how is it that you can speak in the language of humans?" said Soraya in surprise. "You must surely be an enchanted bird!"

"Your brother, the Prince, who understands the speech of animals and birds and was imprisoned by our King, taught me to speak while he was in confinement. I came to his barred window each day for the last week, and he told me that surely someone would be coming to find him, for the white stones he had left in the brass dish at home must have turned black."

"Tell him that I shall be waiting, and I will wear the tattered cloak which I came in, for I would be noticed by the guards if I went out in the garden in my fine clothes," said the Princess.

So the bird flew away and reported to the Prince that his sister was ready to meet him as planned.

"Come, courtiers and guests," said the King of the Crocodile-Hunters after the evening meal that night, when the palace clocks were striking nine, "Let us make merry and have music and drummers so that I may marry my dearly-beloved son to this charming Princess who has just come into our midst."

All the musicians began to play and sing, and laughter rang through the great halls of the palace. The courtiers got up and danced before the Royal Party, and all were gay and merry. During the festivities Soraya slipped away and found her old tattered cloak, which she threw over her fine new clothes, and escaped unseen into the garden. There, beside the fountain, she saw a fluffy-haired white cat. The cat mewed three times as she approached, and as Soraya bent down and stroked her, said in a human voice, "Princess, follow me and I will lead you to the gate where your brother awaits with horses ready saddled."

Soraya quickly followed the cat, and just as the moon went behind a cloud she saw a gate open, and her brother, cloaked for riding, stepped forward and took her hand.

"Come with me quickly, sister," said he, "for we must ride hard to get away from this country of the Crocodile-Hunters before they miss us!"

Swiftly he helped her into the saddle of a fine Arab steed, and leapt on to his own horse. They galloped out of the city and away to the south towards their own country.

When the sun rose they were in well-remembered surroundings, and the Prince said, "Ride bravely for just a little longer, dear sister, for we shall be in our own city by the time the sun is overhead."

Soraya clung to the reins as the mettlesome Arab stallion raced on, his mane and tail flying in the wind. Her mouth was dry and her eyes were sore from the sand borne on the wind, when at last they reached the gates of their own capital.

The Prince rode his horse right up to the great door of the palace, and the servants and maids went down on their knees in happiness and thanksgiving. Soraya and her brother went hand in hand to where their father, the King, turned into stone, sat in the golden throne room.

The Prince bent down and whispered the magic words which the King of the Crocodiles had told him. As he was standing there, fearing that the magic might not work after all, his father opened his eyes and looked about him.

With cries of joy the Queen flung her arms around her husband and told him the whole story from beginning to end.

That night there was a great feast, with the seven Princesses in jewelled dresses; and the King caused all the poor in the kingdom to be fed at the royal table for seven whole days.

The Wise Man
and the Simple Man

ONCE UPON A TIME, in the days of long ago, there lived in Arabia an old Wise Man. He travelled alone, with no one to talk to, and wherever he went people gave him food to help him on his way, and sometimes pieces of cloth with which to patch his cloak. In return he told them stories or gave advice.

One day when he was sitting beside the roadside he was joined by a Simple Man, who sat down beside him.

"Greetings, my son," said the Wise Man. "Are you hungry? Come, share these dates with me."

"Blessings upon you, Master," said the Simple Man, "I have no home and no loved ones left in the world, so may I go with you on your travels?"

"I have nothing to offer, my son," replied the old man, "but you may come with me and stay with me as long as you wish."

For a time they went about contentedly together, and seeing him with the Wise Man, the villagers from round about also fed the Simple Man as they wandered from place to place.

Now, one day the Simple Man picked up a piece of wood from the roadside and said to the old man, "Master, here is a piece of wood you can carve. I have often seen you whittling wood with that very sharp knife of yours. What can you make with this fragment?"

And the Wise Man answered, "Peace, my son, do not ask me what I shall make, something will be suggested."

Days went by, and slowly the fragment of wood grew smaller and smaller as the two went on their way, and everybody who met them asked, "And what are you whittling from that piece of wood, aged sir?"

And the old man gave them all the same answer, "Something will be suggested."

It was now only a very small piece of wood, beautifully carved, and little bigger than a date.

"Master," ventured the Simple Man one day, when they were sitting in a little coffee-shop, sipping sweet golden coffee, "soon there will be nothing left of that piece of wood which you are whittling. What are you making?"

"Patience, my son, something will be suggested," said the Wise Man with a smile.

At that moment a poor woman, who had a crying baby in her arms and a basket of fruit on her head, passed on the way to the market. The day was hot, and the road dusty, and the unfortunate woman was driven nearly frantic by the noise of the child's screams.

As she was passing, with sweat glistening on her face, the Wise Man put out his hand and stopped her. "Wait a second, sister," said he, "I think I have the very thing here for you," and he popped the date-sized piece of carved wood in the baby's mouth. It stopped crying and began to suck contentedly.

"You see, my son," said the Wise Man, as the woman trudged on her way, "unknown to myself I have been making a baby's comforter."

The Warrior's Daughter
and the Three Suitors

ONCE UPON A TIME there lived a man who was a great warrior in the army of Saladin. When he retired from fighting he went with his wife to a far oasis and there they lived in peace for many years.

But one night Abdul Kasim, for such was his name, said to himself: "What use is my life to me if I have no child to carry on my name after I have gone?" and he prayed to Allah that he and his wife could be given a son. But the woman, who was the daughter of a witch, wanted a daughter. So, when a year had passed, by the Mercy of Allah, she gave birth to a son and a daughter. The boy was given the name of Abdul Kerim and the girl was named Zuleika, and they were as alike as two marbles.

The boy grew up, and became a warrior like his father, going away to fight in the wars for the Emir Saladin. The girl became a very beautiful young woman, and her father was so proud of her that he kept her hidden away from all the young men who wanted to marry her, because he thought that she should marry a prince at least.

Poor Zuleika grew weary of the harem, and longed to go

outside the walls of her home. "Mother," said she, "when shall I have the freedom to go out and see the shops in the market, or walk in the cool of the evening under the desert moon?" But her mother said soothingly, "Hush, my child, be at peace, all will be well for you, remember your father knows best."

Now, there were three suitors who came to pay their respects to Abdul Kasim, and they were all young and handsome. They sat in the courtyard of the house all day, and at night time when they went home Abdul Kasim talked with his wife about which one would be suitable.

"Wife," said he, stroking his beard, "I cannot give our daughter to anyone; have I not decided to find a prince to be her husband?"

"Husband," said she, "let me advise you. Tomorrow, when the sun is high in the sky, summon all three young men here and we shall find out which is the most desirable as our son-in-law." So they went to bed and slept.

Next day, when the sun was high in the sky, the three young men returned and sat in the courtyard, each eager to be chosen as the bridegroom of the beautiful Zuleika.

The first young man was a weaver, and he stood up when his name was called by the father.

"Why do you want to marry my daughter, and what can you give her?" asked Abdul Kasim.

"Reverend sir," said the young man, "I am by trade a weaver, and I know all the tricks of the weaver's trade. I can weave the finest white silks from the silk-worm, or the most delicate woollen cloth from the sheep. I will make beautiful cloth for your daughter to wear, and she shall be cool in summer and warm in winter, for my cunning fingers shall spin materials fit for a queen."

"Good," said the old warrior. "Now let me hear the next young man."

"Noble sir," said the second young man, "I am especially skilled in the knowledge of all the animals, and understand the language of animals and birds. Let me have your beautiful daughter and I shall show her the wonders of nature and of the animal

96

world. I can teach her the language of the wild creatures, and she will never be lonely, such kinship will she feel with all Allah's created things."

"Good," said the father. "Now let us hear the other young man."

"Ancient warrior," said the third and last suitor, "let me have your daughter and you shall be proud of your grandsons, for I am a soldier, of a family of soldiers, and in my veins runs the blood of those who died in the battles between our True Believers and the Infidel. I cannot always promise that I shall be at home, but where I go I cannot always choose, for first and foremost I must put my allegiance to the Emir."

Then the old warrior's heart was warmed, and his eyes shone, and he lifted the young man from his knees. "Truly, my son," said he, "you are a worthy husband for my daughter, and I pray that you should be granted many years of life to enjoy it with her and your children!"

And Allah gave them a long and happy life, and sent them many joys. For like must go with like, and so it must be until the end of the world.

The Vanity of the Sultan

ONCE THERE LIVED A SULTAN who was very vain, and he expected everybody who came to his Court to bow down before him.

In vain did the teachers of Koranic law teach that only in Allah was the Power and the Glory. Sultan Kamal thought of himself as the only important being that ever was created.

One day a teacher from another part of Arabia arrived at the palace, and soon the courtiers were listening to his words with great attention. The Sultan heard some of his lecture with interest, then quickly became angry when he saw that the Taleb was not giving him enough respect.

"Stop," said the Sultan, "I wish to hear no more about this subject you are discussing, I notice that you do not bow to me every time you look my way."

"Only in Allah (Whose Name be Exalted!) is that which all men should bow to in reverence," said the Taleb, looking at the ruler with unflinching gaze.

"I am the Shadow of Allah upon Earth!" cried the Sultan, "and I require respect in my unique position."

"All are equal in Islam," said the Taleb simply; "we are all the slaves of the Supreme Being."

"No, no," said the Sultan. "My throne is the Centre of the Earth, the stars in their courses spin around me as the planets round the sun!"

"Be careful, Sultan," said the teacher. "Too much pride will bring you to a fall very soon. This is foolishness, which can only bring disaster."

"Foolishness? Foolishness? You dare to speak like that to me?" shouted the Sultan. "Then you shall be put in prison until such time as you apologise for every word you have uttered!"

He raised his hand, and two soldiers took the Taleb to a prison cell.

Next day, the guards went to take the prisoner some bread and water. Imagine their surprise when they found the cell was empty. The door was locked on the outside, the small, barred window was not big enough to let a mouse out, let alone a man. Yet the Taleb had disappeared without trace.

When the news was taken to the Sultan he became afraid, for he realised that the old man must have been a saint.

"He was sent to give me warning," thought the Sultan to himself. "I must try to remember some of the things he said."

But after a while he forgot all about the mysterious happening and became as vain as ever.

Then at last the Angel of Death came to take Sultan Kamal to Paradise, but the Sultan was not ready to go.

"I have everything which I need in this life," said he, "why should I leave it? When there is all eternity before me, why should my last hour come at this time?"

"It is the Will of Allah," said the Angel of Death. "You should come with a good grace, for Paradise is awaiting you."

Suddenly, the Sultan had a good idea. "I have to go and say my prayers, so I will be in the mosque. Will you please wait for me there?"

"Yes, I shall. When you have finished your prayers you must come with me," replied the Angel.

The Angel vanished, and Sultan Kamal laughed. For he decided never to go into a mosque again. In this way he hoped to avoid the Angel of Death for a long time.

Years passed, and the Sultan forgot all about the visitation of the Angel.

One day the Caliph came to visit him, and it was a Friday, the day of Rest.

"Let us feast together after we have been to the mosque," said the Caliph, "for I have a strong desire to discuss with you a matter of the greatest importance."

The Sultan agreed, and was just about to step inside the mosque when he saw the tall shrouded figure of the Angel of Death standing there. "Stop," said the angel, "you must come with me today, just as soon as you have said your prayers."

Only Sultan Kamal saw the apparition, for he was invisible to all but Kamal. "No, not today," he begged. "The Caliph is about to invite me to a feast, and he has something of great importance to discuss."

"You have kept me waiting long enough," said the Angel. "You shall come today, for it is written."

"Very well then," said the Sultan. "Let me say my last prayer to Allah for forgiveness, and I will come with you," and he fell upon his knees. When he had finished, he rose, and the Angel of Death put a cold hand upon his arm. Sultan Kamal felt himself being lifted through the air as if he weighed no more than a feather, and he said, "Take me to Paradise, I have to go sooner or later, I suppose."

"No, not so," came the chill words of the shrouded Angel. "You cannot be taken to Paradise after your refusal to come with me when I visited you before. Then, you could have gone to the Everlasting Garden, but now, now it is Allah's Decree that you go to the Lower Regions of fire and flame."

So, the congregation at the mosque rose from their knees at the end of the prayers to find the Sultan Kamal, at the height of his greatness, lying lifeless on the marble floor.

The Princess
and the Mouse

ONCE UPON A TIME there lived the daughter of a king. Her name was Safia. Her father and mother loved her very much, and would deny her nothing in the world.

One day, a magician came to the palace and asked for sanctuary, saying that he was a professor who was being persecuted by his enemies and had nowhere to write an important book.

"Good professor," said the King, "you shall have a room placed at your disposal and everything that you desire, in order that you may finish your great work."

So the magician went on with his spells and magic formulas, pretending to be engrossed in scholarly matters. Every Friday, which was the day of rest in that far land, the magician paid his respects to the King and his court, but secretly he desired to take away the King's throne.

One day he disguised himself as an old woman and walked under the trees in the palace gardens till he met Safia.

"Princess," he said, "let me be your laundress, for I can wash linens and silks as finely as anyone in the world, and I would do it for almost nothing if I could serve Your Highness."

103

"Good woman," said the Princess Safia, "I can see that you are a poor creature and grieve for your condition. Come to my private quarters and I shall give you some of my linen to wash."

So the disguised magician followed the princess into the palace, and before the girl could see what was happening he bundled her into a laundry bag and ran away as fast as his legs would carry him. He took the Princess into his private room. Muttering a magic spell, he made her as small as a doll, and put her in a cupboard.

The next Friday he went to the court as usual, and found the whole palace in uproar. "The Princess Safia has vanished, and His Majesty is nearly out of his mind. All the soothsayers have tried to find out through their magical powers where she can be, but none of them have managed it," said the Grand Vizier.

The wicked magician smiled, for he knew that his spell was so strong it would defy all the soothsayers in the land until the day of his death.

The next day passed, and the Queen was weeping in her bower when the magician entered, disguised as a washer-woman. He put her into a laundry bag and took her into his private room. She was turned into a doll no bigger than his thumb.

"Ha-hah!" laughed the magician, "I will now go and capture the King, and will rule the country myself."

So, next day, he waited until the King had gone to rest, tired out with worrying about the Queen's disappearance, and disguised in his usual way, he captured the King also. He turned the King into a doll no bigger than the Queen, and shut him up in the cupboard too.

Now, with their royal family gone, all the courtiers began to weep and wail, and came to the magician's study in a large party to beg for his advice.

"You are a learned man," said the Grand Vizier, "you must know a lot of things. Will you please tell us what to do?"

"Until your King and Queen and Princess come again, let me be your ruler," said the magician, and the people agreed. So for a long time the wicked magician ruled over the people and gathered much wealth, for they brought him all the gold in the country. Every now and again he would send out troops to search the length and breadth of the land for news of the missing King and his wife and daughter. But, of course, there was no sign of them.

Now, one day a mouse found its way into the cupboard where the Princess Safia was hidden, and got the surprise of its life when she said, "Mouse, mouse, eat a hole in this cupboard so that I can escape, for the wicked magician who turned me into this shape will never let me out, and I shall die."

"Who are you?" asked the mouse.

"My father is the King, and will reward you handsomely. You shall have free cheese for the rest of your life," said the Princess.

"Allah have mercy!" said the mouse. "His Majesty the King has disappeared, and so has the Queen, and the magician is on the throne."

"Oh no," wept the Princess, "what has happened to them? Can the wicked magician have captured them too?"

"Wait here," said the mouse, "and I will have a look in the rest of the cupboard." And sure enough, he found the King and Queen, turned into tiny dolls, on the top shelf. But in their case they were stiff as if they have been carved out of wood, because the magician had cast a different spell upon them.

The mouse went back and told the Princess the sad news.

"Alas, alas," the Princess cried, "what am I to do then, for even if I do escape what will happen to me?"

"Princess," said the mouse, "I will help you. I will go and see a Wise Woman who lives in a hollow tree, and tonight I shall come back and tell you what she says."

So the Princess hid once more in the cupboard, and the mouse scuttled off.

Inside a large tree which had seen many winters there lived an old Wise Woman, and the mouse went to her, saying "Mother, tell me what I should do to help the King's daughter who has been turned into a doll by the magician. She hopes to escape through a hole I shall nibble in a cupboard door. I have discovered that our missing King and Queen are also in the same cupboard, turned into wooden dolls no bigger than your thumb."

105

"Tell the King's daughter that she must come here when the moon is up and I will help her," said the Wise Woman.

The mouse went back when it was night and nibbled the wood away until it was possible for Safia to get through the hole. As she was so small, it was easy for the Princess to run with the mouse out of the palace without being seen by the guards. When the moon rose and the garden was flooded with light, the tiny Princess went to a cavity in the tree which the mouse had showed her, and peeped in.

"Enter, King's daughter," said the Wise Woman. "I have found out by looking in my magic books the answer to your problem." The mouse waited nearby to see that no one was coming, and Safia sat on a footstool as the old woman read from a large volume of magic.

"You must go on until you reach the crossroads, and in a field near by you will see an orange-coloured horse, already saddled and bridled for a journey. Jump on his back, after giving him a magic grass-seed to eat."

"Where shall I get the magic grass-seed?" asked the Princess.

"I will give it to you," said the Wise Woman, looking into a drawer.

"What am I to do after I have caught the horse?" asked Safia.

"King's daughter, you must whisper into his ear, 'Take me, Orange Horse, to where the sacred pear tree grows, so that I may bring away a pear from its topmost branch,' " said the old woman, putting her book back on the shelf.

"And then shall I regain my proper size?" asked the Princess.

"When the wicked magician is dead and not before shall you turn back into your normal size," said the Wise Woman. "You must mount the orange horse's back once more and ride until you reach the Well of the Green Ogre. Whisper into the horse's right ear and you will arrive there before you know it. Drop the pear right into the depths of the well, for the wicked magician's soul is hidden in that pear, and if it falls into the ogre's den it will be devoured by the ogre, and the magician will die."

"What will happen then?" the Princess wanted to know.

"After that, all the creatures turned into other shapes by the

106

magician will return to their own forms, and all will be as it was before." And the Wise Woman put a grass-seed into her hand.

So the tiny Princess thanked the Wise Woman, said good-bye to the mouse, and ran on in the moonlight until she reached the crossroads.

She saw, just as the old woman had said, a horse which was the colour of an orange, with a beautiful golden mane and tail, standing in the field, ready saddled and bridled.

"Orange horse! Orange horse!" called Safia in a low voice. "Here is a magic grass-seed. Take me to the tree where the sacred pears grow, so that I may pick the topmost pear from its branches."

So the orange-coloured horse put its head down close to Safia, and she held out the seed, which he swallowed. Then he put his head down again so that she could climb on to his neck, clinging to the golden mane. Soon she was hanging on to the saddle for all she was worth. The horse neighed twice, then, tossing his head, galloped away like the wind.

In less time than it takes to tell, Safia found herself in a beautiful orchard where there were cherry trees, plum trees, and trees with mulberries upon them, but only one pear tree.

"Here it is," said the horse; and standing on the saddle Safia stretched up into the branches. She picked a pear from the topmost branch and put it carefully into the saddlebag.

"Take me to the Well of the Green Ogre," she whispered in the horse's right ear. The orange-coloured horse nodded and was off like the wind, his hooves moving so fast they seemed never to touch the ground. There, beside three palm trees, was a well. In the moonlight Safia saw that just inside the well there was an ogre's head as big as a pumpkin, with huge round eyes and a large mouth. She hurriedly took the pear containing the soul of the magician out of the saddlebag and dropped it right into the Green Ogre's mouth. Instantly he chewed the pear up into tiny pieces, and Safia suddenly found herself growing. She was her own size again - the wicked magician was dead.

The horse took her back to the crossroads, and just as she was about to thank him, there was a clap of thunder and he disappeared before her eyes.

She hurried to the palace, and then to the room where she knew her mother and father were imprisoned. She found the King and Queen were their normal size again, but very puzzled indeed to find themselves in a cupboard. She quickly explained.

"Call the Captain of the Guard!" the King commanded. "Have the magician arrested, and his head shall be struck from his shoulders."

But when the soldiers went to the royal bedchamber to find the false king, they discovered that he was dead, for the moment the Green Ogre had eaten the pear he had perished, as the Wise Woman had predicted.

That day there was great rejoicing in the palace, and Safia went to thank the Wise Woman who lived in the hollow tree. But of the tree there was no sign - it had vanished as if it had never been. Safia could scarcely believe her eyes, and was looking round in a puzzled way when she was approached by a tall, handsome young man, dressed in fine clothes.

"Blessings upon you, dear Princess," said he, "for I was the mouse, a victim of enchantment, who nibbled the hole through which you escaped to go upon that journey to find the pear which contained the magician's soul."

"So it was true, and not a dream!" cried Safia. "I came to find the Wise Woman and she has gone."

"She lived in an enchanted tree," explained the young man, "and now that she wishes to be elsewhere the tree has been uprooted and taken there without leaving a sign behind."

"Come with me to my father so that he can thank you," cried Safia.

So the young man went with her, and when they knelt before the King he explained that he was a prince who had been turned into a mouse by the magician.

"You shall stay here and marry my daughter," promised the King, "and rule the kingdom after me, as I have no son."

And so it came to happen, and the wedding feast was celebrated for seven days and seven nights, and Safia and her husband lived happily ever after.

The Three Deaf Men
and the Dumb Dervish

ONCE UPON A TIME there was a goatherd, who was very deaf. One day, having taken his goats to where there was plenty for them to eat, he remembered that he had left his food behind in the village where he lived. His wife had handed him the bundle, but he had forgotten it. He waited until midday, when the sun beat down on his head; his wife had not sent the child with his meal, so he realised that she had not known he had left it.

Now, working not far from him, with a sharp cutting tool, was a man gathering some shrubs for his horse. So the goatherd approached him and said:

"Brother, would you kindly keep an eye on my goats while I go home for my food? I left it at home this morning, and my wife hasn't sent the child with it, so I must go back for it. I shall not be long, so would you please see the goats don't wander?"

Now, the man gathering the shrubs was also very deaf, and he did not understand a word the goatherd said, so he answered: "Why, I need all this which I am cutting for my own horse, I certainly will not give it to you for your goats! Go on, and leave me in peace!" And he waved his arms about in great excitement.

The goatherd, thinking that he was agreeing, thanked him and ran off towards the village. The shrub-cutter continued his work.

When he got home, the goatherd looked for his wife, to give her a telling off about letting him go off without his food. But the poor woman was lying on her bed, suffering from a sudden fever, and was in such a sorry state that he forgot all about scolding her. A neighbour's wife was looking after her and the child, so he picked up his bundle of bread and dates, and returned to his flock.

Now, having eaten his meal, and feeling grateful to the man for looking after his goats, he thought to himself, "I really ought to reward this good man for keeping an eye on the animals while I was away. If he hadn't been here goodness knows what might have happened to them! I will give him this lame goat which is no use to me, he will be able to roast it and have a feast tonight." So putting the injured goat on to his back, he went up to the man and said, "Here is a present for you, for looking after the flock while I went home to the village. Alas, my poor wife had a fever when I got there, so I was not able to scold her for letting me forget my food."

The deaf shrub-cutter, seeing the goatherd coming with the animal, thought that the other was complaining about the goat's injured leg and said, "Why should you be so dismayed with this turn of events? Can I possibly be to blame because your wretched creature broke its leg? I was not even looking in that direction, how can I do anything about the accident?"

"My dear friend," said the goatherd, "it is a fine young animal, and will make a delicious stew for you and your family!"

"I tell you," shouted the shrub-cutter, "I never went near them, it is no good telling me about it! Get along with you, I have no more time to stand here gossiping with you, vile goatherd!"

Seeing that the other man was in a temper, the goatherd dropped the kid on to the ground and began to shout too, trying to make himself heard. As they were going at it angrily, a traveller on the road came up to see what was happening. He got off his horse and led it towards the two men.

The goatherd said, "I was just trying to give this man a young tender goat as a present for looking after my flock of goats while I went home to the village, but he seems to take it as some sort of insult!"

The traveller put a hand behind his ear and the shrub-cutter said: "This wretched goatherd blames me because one of his creatures seems to have broken a leg while I was here but I did not even look in that direction for the last hour!"

By a curious trick of Fate, the traveller, too, was deaf, and he thought both were saying something which concerned him. He answered:

"Yes, this horse does not really belong to me, I caught him some way up the road, and as I was tired, I mounted and rode this far. I'm sorry if it belongs to you, please accept my apologies, I herewith return it with many thanks."

At this moment, an ancient Dervish happened to be passing, and the three men begged him to judge their case.

Now the Dervish could hear them all perfectly well, but he was unable to speak, for he was dumb.

So he looked at each man steadily for a full minute, his dark brilliant eyes holding theirs in an almost hypnotic gaze.

After all the shouting and excitement, this had a most peculiar effect on the three deaf men. Fear overtook them, for they began to imagine that the Dervish had some strange and mystic power which might cause them to be bewitched.

Fearing that something awful was going to happen, the man who had caught the horse mounted it and rode quickly away.

The shrub-cutter gathered up all the fodder he needed and piled it in his net, hoisting it on to his back, and trudged off.

Still the Dervish looked on with his unblinking stare, so the goatherd decided to drive his goats a bit farther on to better grazing. Then the Dervish, going quietly on his way, thought to himself that in many ways the gift of speech was one that human beings could easily have done without.

The Rich Merchant,
the Poor Merchant and the Jinn

ONCE UPON A TIME there lived in Basra two men who had grown up together, called Ibrahim and Yusuf.

Now, Ibrahim had become a rich merchant, and had the most wonderful good fortune in everything. But Yusuf, though also a merchant, had nothing but bad luck; he lost some of his best ships at sea, and could not make up the losses. He was almost penniless, and did not know what to do for money.

The rich merchant was always trying to impress others with his importance. He had no pity on his poor friend, and never thought of helping him in his difficulties.

Poor Yusuf was going home late one night, when he fell into a hole in the road which had been left by some careless workmen. He called out several times, but there was nobody to hear. After a while, he shouted again, and a voice said: "Hold on to my hands, and I will help you." At the same moment he felt some-one seize his fingers.

It was dark, and Yusuf could not see who it was who spoke, but he gripped the hands, which seemed very strong, and was soon out of the hole.

"Thank you, may Allah reward you," said Yusuf, and tried to see his rescuer in the darkness. "Who are you, and how can I repay you?"

"I am a Jinn," came the reply, "and I will be satisfied if you will do me a small favour."

"A Jinn?" cried Yusuf in alarm. "What sort of a Jinn?" He knew that there were all kinds of Jinn, good and bad, and that some of them could make human beings their slaves.

"I am a very small Jinn, though I am strong," was the answer. "And I am looking for someone who will do me a small service. All I want you to do is to take me to a certain place, and there I will tell you more."

Thinking that perhaps after all he did owe the Jinn one good turn at least, Yusuf agreed to go with him to a ruined house.

"Here in the wall," said the Jinn, "is a secret hiding-place. Only a man may open it, and for years I have been looking for someone to help me. As soon as I speak to ordinary people they run away. I am glad you are so understanding."

"What do you want me to do?" said Yusuf.

"Lift that stone," said the Jinn, and pointed to a flat slab set in the floor, "and I will go down. Then you shall see."

Yusuf did as he was told, and when the hiding-place beneath the stone was revealed the Jinn disappeared into the opening. He was soon back with a clay pot which was full of gold coins.

"Treasure!" said Yusuf. "How did you know that was there?"

"We Jinn are the guardians of buried treasure, and this one has been known to me for many years. I was once the servant of a magician who lived in this house when it was new, about a hundred years ago. When he died, the secret of his treasure died with him, but I have waited all these years to find it again," said the Jinn. "Wait, I will get more." He disappeared down the hole again. Yusuf was amazed, and he let the coins trickle through his fingers. If only he had some of the gold he could buy more ships, and send them out to foreign countries with his merchandise. The Jinn handed him up another pot of gold.

"You take it," said the Jinn. "Use it as you like, but there is just one other thing I have to ask of you."

114

"And what is that?" said Yusuf.

"You must carry me upon your shoulders wherever you go," said the Jinn. "I am not very big, and I will be no trouble to you. You see, I am now getting weary of walking, and if I give you plenty of gold, which I do not need, all you have to do is to let me sit on your shoulders, with my legs around your neck."

"But I cannot!" said Yusuf. "What would it look like? What would people say? Here, take the gold, I must be off home now."

"It is not as easy as that," said the Jinn. "I can imprison you in this ruined house, here under the floor, if you do not obey me. Now, here am I, the most reasonable of all King Suliman's creatures, making you a fine offer like this, and you are so foolish as to refuse. Come, do as I say."

"No," said Yusuf, "I would rather not. I am grateful to you for helping me when I fell into the hole in the road, but what you ask is impossible. Now, let me go." Yusuf tried to shake himself free, as he felt the Jinn's strong hands round his neck. He pushed with all his might. The Jinn gave a loud cry and fell back into the secret hiding-place. Yusuf quickly put the stone over the hole, and the Jinn was imprisoned. Then gathering up the gold which was in the two pots, Yusuf tied it up in his handkerchief and went home as fast as he could.

Time passed, and Yusuf's luck improved. He invested the gold which he had got from the Jinn and made a good profit. Every day things went better for him, and at last he was almost as rich as his old friend, Ibrahim.

Now, Ibrahim was very jealous of Yusuf's rise to wealth, and wondered how he had done it. So, one night he invited him to a meal, and when they had eaten, he asked, "Come, now, Yusuf, tell me the secret of your good fortune. You must have been very clever."

"Shall we say that I had a great stroke of luck," said Yusuf.

"What sort of luck?" asked Ibrahim. "Do forgive my being so inquisitive, but I would like to know."

Mellowed by the food, and feeling that it could do no harm to tell, Yusuf said at last: "Oh well, I suppose I can tell you. I got

115

the money to begin with from a Jinn."

"Allah! Do you mean to tell me that you have a Jinn? Where is he? How do you conjure him up?" Ibrahim was very excited.

"I do not have anything to do with him, it was only once that I saw him," said Yusuf hastily. "Say no more about it, for I would rather not talk about it."

Ibrahim, however, pestered him so much, that at last he told him the whole story. He described the ruined house, but said, "Do not, I beg you, go near it, or the Jinn may get out, and I shall have him upon my back for ever."

The rich merchant did not believe Yusuf, he imagined that his friend was only trying to put him off. "I will go there tonight on the way home," he thought, "and see if I can get some of this gold for myself. The Jinn will not harm me, I am sure, if I talk to him nicely."

So he said good night, and went out to look for the house which Yusuf had told him about. He found it, and by the light of a lantern he discovered the stone slab under which the treasure was hidden.

"Now I will be able to help myself," he chuckled, "there must be enough gold down there to keep me in luxury for the rest of my life."

He pulled up the stone, and looked down into the hole. It was dark, so he leaned down farther. As far as the eye could see were piles of gold coins, jewels and trinkets, glistening in the light of the lantern.

Suddenly, as he was rubbing his hands in glee, he heard a voice.

It was the Jinn.

"So, you have come to let me out, have you?" said the Jinn. "I have been in here for quite a long time. Thank you, I will repay you by giving you all the gold you want. Let me hand you a pot of coins, and then I shall ask a small favour of you."

"O delightful Jinn," replied Ibrahim, "I will do you any favour which you ask. Just let me have some gold, and I will be your friend for ever."

"And so you shall be," said the Jinn, leaping upon the

116

merchant's back. "Yes, we shall be friends always. All I want you to do in return is to carry me upon your back, for I am now very tired indeed of walking."

And Ibrahim, in exchange for the gold which the Jinn gave him, had to carry him about on his back for the rest of his life!

The Queen of Sabah
and the Infidel

A LONG TIME AGO, there lived in Sabah, Southern Arabia, a great queen called Bilquis.

The European world knows her as the Queen of Sheba. Solomon the Son of David (upon whom be peace!) is said to have married her, and their son was the first King of Ethiopia, but this story is long before that.

Queen Bilquis was sitting one day in her palace being fanned by ten slave girls with ostrich-feather fans, for the day was very hot indeed. Musicians were playing her favourite music, with reed pipes and drums, and there was harmony all around her.

Suddenly, a servant came in and threw himself at the Queen's feet and cried, "Mighty Bilquis, a stranger has been found in the palace grounds and he is to be put to death for daring to profane the streets of Sabah with his infidel presence."

The Queen was interested. "Let him come before me and give a reason for his coming," she said.

The stranger was a wandering scholar from Spain, who had ridden on camel-back all through Arabia. He was lucky enough to have learned the Arabian language, and had easily made his way so far south. But now the fierce warriors of Sabah had seized him and wanted to put him upon the executioner's block for entering the city of their Queen.

When he was brought before Bilquis, she was pleased at his appearance. He was tall and sunburned, wearing a white *burnous* of camel hair, and had brown eyes which smiled boldly at everyone.

"What is your name," asked the Queen, "and what is your business?"

"My name is Tomas Garcia," said he, "and I am a traveller from Spain who has been interested for years in the exploration of Arabia."

"You speak our language well," said Queen Bilquis, "but that will not save you from death. My people are True Believers, and will not allow any Infidel in this city, however well they can make themselves understood."

"I did not know I was so far out of my way," said Tomas. "For two days my camel and I were forced to lie in the sand while a violent sandstorm sprang up in the Empty Quarter. My instruments for discovering my position were lost and I let the animal have its head. It brought me here."

"If you will become a Moslem," said the Chief Minister, "then you could stay here safely. We could not then shed your blood. What do you say to that, Infidel?"

"No," said Tomas, "I have found my own religion enough in my life so far, and can only serve one God!"

"Allah is the Supreme Being above all others!" cried a doctor of religious law. The Chief Minister spoke in the Queen's ear. She smiled.

"Tomas Garcia," she said, "if you can answer one question, then you shall have your life, and go wherever you wish.

"If in three days' time you can give the correct answer to the question you are a free man. If you cannot answer, then you shall die. That is my command."

"What is the question, O Queen?" asked Tomas.

"Where is the centre of the Earth?" said the Queen, then turning to the Chief Minister, she said, "Bring him back in three

120

days' time for his answer."

Back in the dungeon, Tomas Garcia thought and thought until his head ached, but he could not think of a suitable reply to the puzzling question. What could the Queen mean? It was obvious to him that he had nothing to look forward to but the executioner's block in three days from now.

That night, he lay uncomfortably on the hard floor of the prison, wrapped in his *burnous*, and struck with his fists on the stones beneath him.

"Oh, unlucky creature that I am," he said aloud. "What misfortune this is, to lose my life for such an innocent misunderstanding like coming to a religious stronghold of blood-thirsty Mohammedans! If only someone could help me so that I might return to Spain safe and sound!"

As he finished speaking a Geni appeared and stood before him with folded arms. "By striking the floor and asking for help you have conjured me up from my long sleep," said the Geni. "I can tell you what it is that Queen Bilquis wants to know."

"By Heaven," said Tomas, jumping to his feet, "how did you appear?"

"Upon the very flagstone which you have touched with your fist is a magical cabalistic sign, carved there by a magician who inhabited this dungeon many years ago," said the Geni. "You brought me to you by touching that sign, and your luck has changed for the better."

"Then get me out of here, and let me be gone," cried Tomas.

"No, I have no power to do that," said the Geni, "but this is the answer to the Queen's question." He bent forward and whispered the words in Tomas's ear.

"Oh, thank you, thank you," said the Spaniard. "How can I ever repay you?"

"I need no repayment, I am immortal and that is enough," said the Geni. "I will now return to my sleep, for I shall not wake again for a hundred years when another mortal in this very dungeon will have need of me. Farewell!"

And he vanished into thin air.

Tomas Garcia lay down again on the floor and slept

peacefully for the rest of the night.

In the morning he wondered if it had all been a dream. In any case, he resolved to try his luck with the answer the Geni had given him when his time should come to go before the Queen.

It seemed a very long time to wait and after a whole day and another night had dragged by, Tomas feared he was never going to see the light of day again.

At last he found himself in the throne room of Queen Bilquis, ready to give his answer.

"Well, Infidel, what have you decided to tell me?" demanded the Queen. "Come, we are all listening. Where is the centre of the Earth?"

All the courtiers held their breath, and there was not a sound in the great throne room as Tomas boldly replied: "Here, under the feet of your throne, Queen of Sabah, is the Centre of the Earth!"

There was a gasp from the Queen, and every eye was on Tomas Garcia as he stood proudly in his white *burnous* before her.

Then Queen Bilquis held out her hand to Tomas and smiled very graciously, for she was pleased and flattered at such a reply.

"The perfect answer," she said, "and the right one. So you, Infidel though you are, shall have three days and nights of rest and hospitality here before being allowed to go upon your way."

So the Geni had been truly helpful and saved Tomas Garcia from an unhappy end.

The Queen of Sabah entertained Tomas to a great feast, and he told her many tales of his travels. Since those far-away days, after Tomas got home, many others tried to visit Sabah but they never found it. To this day that part of the world, beyond the Empty Quarter, is still called "Danger-of-death" or The Hadramaut.

The Ghostly Miser
of Tangier

ONCE UPON A TIME, in the old part of Tangier, in Morocco, there lived a man called Abu Bin Ibrahim. He was a bricklayer and worked very hard to keep a large family.

One day he was building a wall for the garden of a doctor's house. An old man with a long white beard was passing by on the road, and stopped to watch him.

Then he said to the bricklayer: "When you have finished tonight, could you come to my house and do something for me?"

"Certainly, Sidi," said Abu Bin Ibrahim, "tell me the address and I shall call there after the evening prayer."

"No, I cannot do that," said the old man, "for it is a most secret matter and I do not want to disclose the name of the street or the house. But I pay well; for your work there I shall give you one piece of gold, or two, if it takes longer."

"One piece of gold? What sort of work do you want done?" cried Abu Bin Ibrahim.

"Only, bricklaying," was the reply, "but I must come and fetch you, because of the secrecy attached to the affair. Where do you live?"

My home is the last house in the Street of the Scorpion," said the bricklayer. "Everybody knows me there. I will look out for you about eight o'clock."

"Very well," said the bearded man, "I will be there."

He went away, and Abu Bin Ibrahim continued his work and soon forgot all about him. But that night, when he was having his evening meal, he remembered and said to his wife: "I may have to go out later, my dear, I am doing some extra work for someone who is coming here to fetch me. Do not worry if I am not back for some time."

No sooner had he finished talking to his wife than there was a knock on the door.

"Ah," said Abu Bin Ibrahim, "that will be the man who wants me to go and work at his house." Outside, with a lantern, was the old white-bearded stranger.

"Peace be upon you, Sidi," said the bricklayer, and the other answered, "Upon you too be peace." So Abu Bin Ibrahim walked along the street with the old man in the light of the bobbing lantern.

When they got to the end of the narrow lane the old man took a handkerchief out of his pocket and said, "Now I must bind your eyes, for remember it is a secret matter and I cannot tell you where my house is situated."

The bricklayer let the stranger blindfold him, and presently he felt himself being led along, first right and then left, until he quite lost all sense of the direction in which they were walking.

Suddenly they stopped, and Abu Bin Ibrahim felt himself being helped up some steps, and through a doorway. The bandage was removed and he looked about him. He stood in a most beautiful courtyard, with Moorish tiles and carved pillars. There was a tinkling fountain in the centre of the court with sculptured birds and animals of the finest marble.

"What do you want me to do?" the bricklayer asked, wondering whose house they were entering.

"A simple task, such as you do every day," said the old man, and showed Abu Bin Ibrahim a pile of bricks and some mortar. "Merely brick up this opening in the wall, and say nothing about it to anyone you know."

"Very well," said Ibrahim, "I will begin at once."

He took up the trowel and started with a will. There were some sacks piled up in an aperture in the wall and as he brushed against them it seemed to him that he heard a chink as if they were full of coins.

When Abu Bin Ibrahim had finished the job it was nearly dawn. He was rewarded with two pieces of gold and could scarcely believe his eyes. "I would not mind doing this sort of work more often," said Abu Bin Ibrahim, rattling the money in his pocket.

The old man tied a handkerchief once more over his eyes, and led him into the street. "Remember, complete secrecy," he said, as he left Ibrahim at the door of his own house.

Ibrahim arrived just as his wife was getting up.

"Where have you been all night?" she asked anxiously.

"Ask no questions, my dear," said he, putting the gold pieces into her hands. "Do not nag me, for though the work was secret, it certainly was well paid. I cannot divulge anything about it."

And no matter how she pestered him, he did not satisfy her curiosity.

A few days later, Ibrahim was busy working on the wall of the doctor's house when the old white-bearded man appeared again. "Would you like to earn another two pieces of gold for the same sort of task as before?"

"Yes, certainly, Sidi," said Abu Bin Ibrahim. "Will Your Honour call at my house after the evening prayer?"

The old man agreed, and came to Ibrahim's house and blindfolded him.

They went through streets broad and narrow, and up the steps into the house.

When the blindfold was removed, he was in the same beautiful courtyard with the tinkling fountain in the middle.

"Brick up the opening to this small room," said the old man, and Ibrahim saw a chamber with a number of padlocked chests inside. He did as he was told, and when it was dawn the old man paid him as before. Bandaging Ibrahim's eyes, he led him home again by a roundabout way.

"Remember, complete secrecy," he said, as he removed the handkerchief.

"I promise," said the bricklayer, and the old man hurried away.

Years passed and Ibrahim worked hard at his bricklaying. Many a time he wished that some Jinn or Geni would show him some buried gold so that he could buy a house and bring up his children well, instead of in poverty.

He often wondered what had happened to the old man with the long white beard, but he never saw him in the streets or the *souks* of Tangier.

One evening, sitting with some friends in a coffee-house, the talk turned to ghosts and spirits.

"The big house which my mistress has just bought is haunted," said a crony. "For a long time, they say, an old man with a long white beard has been seen there at night-time groaning and wringing his hands."

"Do people know who the house belonged to before your mistress took it?" asked Ibrahim.

"Yes, it was an old gentleman who was said to be very wealthy, but when he died last year there was not one copper piece in the place. He had no relatives or friends, but lived alone there for many years. It is said he was a little strange and rather miserly. My mistress thinks she may have to leave unless someone can get rid of the ghost!"

"An old white-bearded man?" cried Abu Bin Ibrahim. "I believe I did some work once for someone like that. I wonder if it could be the same person? Let me go to the house; I may be able to help your mistress to remove the evil influence."

His friend took him to the old house, and as soon as he entered the courtyard Abu Bin Ibrahim knew it was the same place where he had bricked up the old miser's treasure.

The new owner received him with some surprise when he said he had a plan to exorcise the ghost of the old man who had lived there before her.

"How do you think you can manage it?" she cried. "I have had learned men here, from the most religious Taleb to professors of

126

astrology, and all of them have failed. If you are not successful, then I shall pull the house down. If you are able to free me of the unhappy spirit, you will be well rewarded."

"Leave it to me, lady," said the bricklayer. "Just go and stay at some other house for a few days, and when you come back I can promise you the old man will have gone."

So she went to stay with her aunt, and Abu Bin Ibrahim sat up all night to watch for the ghost.

About midnight there was a loud groaning cry, and the little old man, with tears running down his cheeks, appeared to Ibrahim.

"Alas, alas," he cried. "My gold, my lovely gold, and chests of treasure, all buried and lost, why did I have to leave the world without using it for the benefit of my fellow men? Now I regret bricking it up in my house. If only I had given it away!"

"Greetings, Sidi," said Abu Bin Ibrahim, politely, behaving as if the situation were absolutely normal. "Do not distress yourself so much, I will help you to rest, if you will allow me."

"How can that be?" asked the old ghost. "I cannot rest, for I am bound to the earth by the anxiety over my treasure, and I cannot enjoy the peace which Allah gives to those who have come to the natural end of their lives."

"What would you like me to do with the gold and treasure which is buried here?" asked the bricklayer. "I will obey your instructions, and then you can rest in peace."

"Break down the wall where you bricked up my sacks of gold," said the ghostly old man, "and distribute it to the poor of Tangier. Then, open the small chamber where the chests are hidden, and make a trust for the orphans of Morocco. As for yourself and your family, good Abu Bin Ibrahim, take as much gold as you require to keep yourselves in comfort until the end of your days."

"It shall be done," promised the bricklayer, "just as soon as I can get my chisel and hammer." As he spoke, the old man vanished.

All night long Abu Bin Ibrahim laboured to open the secret hiding-places, and gradually he pulled out the store of gold coins

127

until all the sacks stood in the tiled courtyard. Next day, and the day after, he worked at opening the small room, and dragged the padlocked chests into view. Then he sent for the Kadi, and showed him the wonderful treasure. "The unhappy ghost who haunted this house told me that this hidden money was to be given for the good of the poor, and a trust was to be founded for the orphans of Morocco."

"By the Beard of the Prophet!" cried the Kadi, "I have never in all my life heard such a story! A bequest of so many thousands being made by a ghost!"

"My family and I are also to benefit," said the bricklayer, "for we are to take as much as will keep us for the rest of our lives."

"The owner of the house must have the last word here," said the Kadi. "Send word to the Lady Fatima that the treasure has been found, and ask her to come as soon as she can."

As they were speaking the ghost of the old man appeared again, and this time instead of moaning he seemed to be pleased, as he walked through the courtyard and disappeared through the wall.

When the lady Fatima returned, she gladly gave permission for the money to be distributed. "If the old man's wish is granted," she said, "I am sure that he will no longer be bound to this world, but will be able to enter the Garden of Paradise with a satisfied heart. And my house will be free of him."

She was right, for once the money was divided as he had asked, the ghost never was seen again.

The honest bricklayer and his large family moved into a villa overlooking the sea very shortly afterwards. The days of hard work and grinding poverty were over for Abu Bin Ibrahim, and he was able to sit in his garden and enjoy the flowers.

The Goldsmith's Daughter
and the Prince of Darkness

ONCE UPON A TIME there lived in the city of Damascus a goldsmith who made items of jewellery so finely that his fame spread even to the ears of Eblis, the Evil One. The goldsmith was sitting in his shop one day, finishing the wings of a golden butterfly, when he saw the dark-eyed Evil One looking through the window.

"Allah have mercy upon me!" cried the goldsmith. "Has my last hour come?"

The door opened as if by magic and the tall, black-robed figure entered. The Evil One smiled and said, "No, good fellow, have no fear. I have not come to carry you off. I was merely looking at your wonderful handiwork, for I have heard, even in the lower regions, of your exquisite craftsmanship. I would like to have some samples; shall we say the few pieces which you have here in the window?"

"Why, yes, yes, certainly. Have all you please," said the goldsmith willingly, for he was so glad to hear the Evil One was going to spare him that he did not mind the loss of his show pieces. "I will wrap them up and you shall take them at once.

There is a jewelled bear, a golden fish with ruby eyes..."

"No, no," said the Evil One, impatiently, "I do not want them now. I will come back for them another time. Keep everything in the window for me. Now remember, promise, even though I may be years in returning!"

"I promise," replied the goldsmith, and the Evil One vanished.

"Who was that talking to you?" asked the goldsmith's wife, bringing her husband a cup of coffee.

"My dear," said he, "it was Eblis the accursed Evil One himself. He made me promise to keep everything which I have in the window for him, and he will be back to collect the items when he is ready. Though I grieve for my beautiful pieces of handiwork, I am grateful that thanks to the Mercy of Allah he has not carried me off to Jehenna!"

"Everything in the window?" said his wife.

"That was what the Evil One wanted," said he.

At that moment the goldsmith's wife clapped her hands to her head and began to weep. "Alas, alas, our child was playing in the window, and there is no doubt that the Evil One means to come and take her too, when he returns!"

The goldsmith rushed to have a look and, sure enough, there was his little daughter, innocently playing with the golden toys which her father had put on show.

"Quick, wife," said he, "go to the silversmith and bring me an ounce of virgin silver."

His wife did as she was bid, and brought back the silver. The goldsmith went to his workshop, and taking the holy Koran from the bookshelf, read a verse from it. Then he hammered out the silver as thin as paper and engraved a talisman for his daughter to wear around her neck as protection. For he knew that a charm was much more potent if worked in silver, and he told his daughter that she must never take the talisman from her neck, or Eblis would carry her away.

Years passed, and still the Evil One did not come back. The goldsmith and his wife had almost forgotten about the whole matter, when the Evil One appeared again in the goldsmith's shop.

"I have come for my treasures, as you promised," said the Evil One. "And the girl is now about seventeen years old, is she not?"

"Yes," said the goldsmith, "but change your mind, O Mighty Eblis, about our daughter. We have no other child in our old age, so please, I beg you, spare her, spare her! Or take me instead. I am beyond the pleasures of life, but she is young. Take me, great Prince of Darkness!"

"No, no, no. I cannot possibly do that," said the Evil One, snatching the beautiful golden figures which the goldsmith handed him. "I want her especially..."

So the goldsmith sent the servant to ask his daughter to come, as she was required urgently in the shop.

Now the girl, whose name was Zorah, was taking a bath, and in her haste to obey her father, she jumped out of the water and, hurriedly drying herself, forgot to put her silver talisman around her neck. She dressed quickly, and ran to the shop. She was surprised to see a tall, dark stranger there, and something about him made her shrink.

"Zorah, my child," said the goldsmith, "this is Eblis, the Evil One, who has come to take you away with him. Now, you cannot go with him against your will, for you are protected by that silver talisman which I placed round your neck when you were small, so have no fear."

"What! How dare you trick me?" cried the Evil One. "I will not be robbed like this!" and he reached out his hand to grasp the girl's clothing, but she ran away from him so fast that she left her veil in his claw-like fingers.

Zorah ran as quickly as her feet would carry her, for she remembered leaving her talisman beside the bath. She heard the Evil One coming close behind her, but just as he was about to catch hold of her, she picked up her talisman chain and threw it over her head. The Evil One gave a cry of rage, and said to the goldsmith, "All right, I am going now, but I will be back for your daughter in seven days, believe me!" and vanished.

Now, the goldsmith had a plan, and it was this. He would make a waxen model of his daughter, and cleverly conceal a machine inside the body, so that it could walk and talk like a human being. He worked secretly, in a cellar, for seven days and nights, until he had made a life-like reproduction of his daughter, perfect to the last detail. Then, having sent his real daughter to her aunt in a distant town, the goldsmith awaited his diabolical visitor.

Sure enough, as he was sitting in his workshop the Evil One appeared once more, and said in sepulchral tones: "Bring your daughter hither this instant, old man, or I will set some of my fiends to burn your house down! I am in no mood to be trifled with at the moment."

So the goldsmith put his head behind the curtains which led to the women's apartments and said: "Zorah my child, come out at once. The mighty Eblis, Prince of Darkness, has come to take you away with him and he is not to be trifled with tonight, or he will set his fiends to burn the house down."

When she heard her husband's voice, the goldsmith's wife turned the key in the back of the beautiful life-sized doll which the goldsmith had made, and arranged a rose-pink veil over its head. "I hear and obey, father," she said in a gentle voice, and parted the curtains, giving the doll a push. She then hid herself behind the door.

The goldsmith held his breath as he saw the model gliding softly into the room. When Eblis, the Evil One, glimpsed the lovely shrouded figure he called, "Come to me now, beautiful creature, so that I may take you with me to my wonderful kingdom of darkness. There you shall be queen of eternal night." He pulled off the veil, and saw a pair of gleaming eyes with long curling lashes.

The voice of the doll murmured softly: "I am transported with delight to be going with you, Great Prince of Darkness. Take me now, and let me live in the Everlasting Fiery Kingdom with you, for ever."

So the Evil One snatched the life-like wax image up in his arms and bore it away to the lower regions, still thinking it to be the beautiful Zorah.

Now, that night there was a gigantic feast in the kingdom of everlasting fire, for Eblis had previously instructed his minions to prepare everything of the finest for the entertainment of his fair bride. Unfortunately, though the food was wonderful, and the wine perfect, the fire was just a little too hot. So, while the Evil One was drinking and laughing on his ebony throne, the lovely wax maiden began to wilt. The fiends put more fuel on the fire, and the doll fell forward as the flames leapt higher. Suddenly, it slipped into the fire and was devoured in an instant. The fiends stood aghast, and leaned on their pitchforks, wondering how their devilish master was going to take his loss. When one of their number went to tell him, he called out, "Well, these human beings are a hopeless lot. Fancy that girl burning up when she had only been here a few hours. How did she think she was going to last down here with me for all Eternity?"

And then the party became merrier and merrier, and the wine flowed like water, while the flames of the great fire crackled louder than ever before. The festivities went on far into the night, and the Evil One never thought of Zorah again.

The Tale of the Rope-maker
and the Sheikh

ONCE UPON A TIME there was a poor rope-maker, who lived with his wife and children in the city of Baghdad.

One evening there came to the rope-maker's shop a rich Sheikh who was a fine talker, with his friend who was a good listener.

While buying a piece of rope, the rich Sheikh said to his friend: "You know, what I was saying earlier is true. People make their way in life because of some chance meeting with Destiny, some financial gain or opportunity which changes the whole course of events."

"Explain further," said the second Sheikh, "I am all attention."

"Take this poor maker of rope, now," said the first Sheikh. "If he had enough money, he could employ others to make rope for him. His family would be properly fed, and his life would be much happier."

"I could not help overhearing what Your Honour was saying," said the rope-maker. "I agree with everything you say, so do forgive me if I ask how I am likely to get a sum of money such as I would need in order to get others to work for me?"

"Allah has been good to me," said the first Sheikh, "and I have been able to gather a great amount of gold which does not benefit me at all, for a man has only one stomach, and can eat only one meal at a time. Now, wherever I see the need I try to alleviate it, and if I can help you with such money as you require to make yourself into a successful employer of rope-makers, then allow me to do so."

The rope-maker could scarcely believe his own ears, and begged the Sheikh to repeat his words.

On hearing them a second time, the rope-maker began to estimate how much money he would need, if he were to enlarge his business.

When he mentioned the sum, the Sheikh took from his inner pocket a bag of gold coins, which came to the total required.

"Thank you a thousand times," cried the rope-maker, "I promise you, generous Sheikh, that I shall make good, and prosper. Your kindness will not go unnoticed by the Angel who records good deeds and..."

"Peace," said the Sheikh, "say no more; we may return in a few months' time to see how Fortune has dealt with you."

Then the two Sheikhs went away.

The rope-maker, whose name was Nurudin, wondered where he might hide the money for the night against thieves, for he knew that in his tiny shop such an amount of money would be seen by any rascal who happened to break in during the night. So, he put it in a jar which contained flour, and covered the gold pieces completely with flour.

Not saying anything to his wife, he went out to a coffee-shop, and thought about his great good fortune.

"I will employ four good fellows who know the trade well," he was thinking to himself as he sipped his coffee, "and then we shall make so much fine rope that we will get a contract from the Caliph. After that our fortunes will be made, and poverty will be a thing of the past for all of us."

That night, Nurudin went home late from the coffee-house, and slept the sleep of one whose life's dream was soon to be reality. Next morning, he went into the shop, and found that the flour-jar was gone.

136

"Wife," he cried in a rage, "where is the flour-jar which stood in this corner last night?"

"Why," she said, "I have given it to the barber's wife in exchange for some henna for dying my hair: I have a few grey hairs which I wanted to hide."

"Woman!" said he, "you have lost us a fortune! I hid a sum of money there which was to make us rich. Go to the barber's wife and get it back at once!"

The rope-maker's wife went to the barber's wife, but the flour-jar had just changed hands.

"I have sold it to a travelling man," said she, "for a new lamp-wick which I needed very badly."

The poor woman went back to her husband, and told him the news.

He was very upset, and sat morosely in his shop for days.

When the generous Sheikh and his friend came back, they looked in some surprise to see Nurudin in the same poor conditions as when they came before.

"An awful accident befell the money you so kindly gave me," said Nurudin, and he told them what had happened.

"Do not worry," said the Sheikh, "that was indeed a misfortune for you, but here is another amount which you should put to good use and try to better yourself once more."

"I cannot take it," cried Nurudin. "It would be unfair to do so, how can I ever repay the other money which was lost?"

"Please do as I ask," said the Sheikh. "I have been given money in this life in order to help others, otherwise how can I be happy?"

So Nurudin took the money, and this time he told his wife about it, and tied it in the corner of his turban. He hid the turban under the bed and went to sleep, to dream of greater riches all night.

Now, in the wall near the bed there was a hole, and in that hole there lived a rat. In the middle of the night, the rat came out, and began to drag the turban into the hole, as she thought it would make a good nest for her young ones.

The turban was heavy, weighed down with the gold, so the

female rat squeaked for the male rat, and together they dragged the turban with its precious load to their den.

In the morning, the poor rope-maker woke up, looked under the bed for his turban, and not finding it, began to wail.

His wife could not understand what the trouble was about, and she began to cry.

"Silence, woman," cried the rope-maker, "the gold has been stolen from under our bed while we lay asleep. How low will these thieves stoop? What shall I do now? The money has gone for the second time!"

When, later on that week, the Sheikh and his friend came to see how the rope-maker was getting on, they could scarce believe their ears. "What! You have lost the second lot of money too?" asked the generous man, "but that is ridiculous! It would appear, from these signs, that Allah does not want you to have a business of your own and riches; I think that I had better not offer you any more money, for it would probably go the way of the other."

Now it was the turn of the other Sheikh to speak. "I have no money to give you," he said, "but here is a piece of lead which I have just picked up in the street. Take this, it may be of use to you at some time, base metal as it is."

Then the two Sheikhs saluted Nurudin, and went their way.

Nurudin took the lead weight home, and put it on the mantel-piece. He was too depressed to say anything about the loss of the money, so he went to bed to try and forget his worries in sleep.

As he tossed and turned, his wife was doing some sewing and she sat up very late with their one lamp, mending his trousers.

The children were all asleep, and it was nearly midnight when there was a knock at the door. "Husband, husband," said the woman, "there is someone at the door at this time of night. Do go and see who it is, for it may be someone in trouble."

"Is there no peace in this world?" said the rope-maker crossly, getting up and opening the door.

Outside the house stood the wife of a fisherman who lived a few houses away.

138

"Good neighbour," said she, "my husband is preparing his net for tomorrow morning's work and finds he is a weight short. Can you, from the goodness of your heart, lend us a piece of metal of any sort which can be used?"

So the rope-maker gave her the lead which he had been given by the Sheikh, and she went away praising him to the skies.

Next day at dawn the fisherman cast his nets and brought in a good harvest of fish. There was so much that he felt sure the lead weight which Nurudin had sent had brought him luck.

"Wife," said the fisherman, "take this big fish to Nurudin with my heartfelt thanks, and say that Allah will reward him in due time."

The woman took one of the best fish caught that morning to the rope-maker's house and the whole family came to admire the fish as it lay on the kitchen table.

The rope-maker's wife cut up the fish to put in the pot, and found inside it a bright stone which gleamed as if it had an inner light.

"That is a strange stone," said she, and, looking at it, decided it would do for the children to play with.

That night there was no oil for the lamp, but the stone which was on the table made the room as bright as if the sun were at the window, even at midnight; and when the fish was cooked, it was as delicious as any they had tasted.

Next day, a woman who was passing the house, paused, and then came to the door. "Good neighbour," said she, "I wonder what sort of light it was you had in your room last night, for my husband and I looked in as we were going home and saw a strange glow. It is so extraordinary that you should have something like that, for we thought you were poor and needy. Has Allah mended your fortunes?"

"Sister," said the rope-maker, "in Allah alone is the Power and the Glory! Our friend the fisherman gave us a large fish from his catch yesterday morning, and last night we found this peculiar stone in the fish's inside. It seems to burn by itself without oil or light, yet we cannot find the reason for this."

"Sell me the stone," said the woman, "and I shall give you

anything you ask. My daughter is sick at home, and I would like to buy it to amuse her."

"My children will cry if I sell it," said the rope-maker's wife, "they have no other toy and I gave it to them when I found it yesterday."

"I will give you fifty pieces of gold," cried the neighbour, "my daughter will recover the minute she sees it, I know she will! Come, give me the wretched thing, so that I may get away about my other business."

"No," said the wife of the rope-maker, for she began to suspect that the stone must be more valuable than she had realised. "I cannot sell it before consulting my husband and he is out at the moment. So if you come back tomorrow, I will tell you what he says."

The other woman went away, very disappointed, and Nurudin's wife told her husband all about it when he returned.

"We must have got something very extraordinary, that someone should offer fifty pieces of gold for it like that," said he. "When the woman comes back, tell her I will not sell at any price!"

Sure enough, the woman returned next day, and bargained with the rope-maker's wife until midday. By then, the price had risen to a hundred pieces of gold, and the visitor showed no signs of going away.

The rope-maker came to the window and called down, more to get rid of the woman than anything: "A thousand gold pieces, take it or leave it!"

"Done," exclaimed the woman, and called to a man who stood in the shadows, "Kemal, bring a thousand pieces of gold from my house, and hurry, for this is a matter which cannot wait!"

Within half an hour, the astonished rope-maker had a bag of gold containing a thousand pieces in his hand and the woman had the glowing stone.

She was just about to go away, when the rope-maker asked, "Tell me, Lady, now you have bought the stone, why were you so keen to get hold of it?"

The woman laughed, and said, "Now I have bought it, of

course I can tell you - this is a stone from a crown of King Suliman, Son of David (upon whom be peace!), and it gives the owner the power to collect riches!"

Then she disappeared.

"It certainly brought us luck," said the rope-maker's wife, as her husband counted his treasure, and they spent all that day making plans for opening a new business.

Within a few weeks Nurudin was the master of a new rope-making establishment. His wife and children had new clothes and as much food as they could eat. Nurudin had given several rope-makers as much work as they could carry out, and made arrangements to sell their output to the Caliph's palace, to the merchants of Baghdad and porters in the market-place. In short, he became the seller of rope to high and low, and soon made a lot more money than he had ever had in his whole life.

When he had the wall of his old shop pulled down, the workmen found the turban which the rats had dragged away, with a few young rats inside it. But, what is more, the gold which the Sheikh had given Nurudin was there safe and sound. No sooner had this been discovered, than Nurudin's wife came hurrying in to say that the travelling man who sold lamp-wicks had brought the jar of flour back, and had returned the money which was hidden in the flour.

"How mysterious are the workings of the ways of Allah!" said Nurudin. "Once I had nothing, now everything comes to me at once. It is almost too much - life is either all or nothing!"

"We must give the wick-seller a reward for bringing the money back," said the wife. "Come, speak to him yourself."

"Friend," said Nurudin, "once someone gave me a chance and put me on the road to success. Take the gold which you have so honestly returned and start yourself some business, which, if Allah wills, may be as prosperous to you as mine is now to me."

"Nurudin," said the wick-seller, "you have spoken well, that is just the sort of answer I was hoping you would give." And at that moment Nurudin saw that the wick-seller was none other than the rich Sheikh who had given him the gold in the first place.

"Who are you?" he asked. "Are you an angel or a Jinn?"

"It does not matter who or what I am," said the Sheikh with a smile. "Enough to say that you have been tried, and are a worthy man. May you be fortunate in your life, and testify to the Greatness of Allah's Wisdom." And so saying the Sheikh vanished from Nurudin's sight.

The rope-maker lived to a ripe old age, and Allah sent him happiness and peace.

The Caliph's Deception

THE CALIPH, Haroun Al Raschid, wandering one evening through the streets of Baghdad, saw a man lying asleep.

"Jaffer," said the Caliph to his Vizier, who was with him, "what a shame it is that this poor fellow should have to lie out here in the street. Has he no home, no money to get a lodging for the night?"

Jaffer bent down, looked through the pockets of the sleeper and found he was penniless.

"Look, Caliph," said the Vizier, "this man has features exactly like those of Your Highness. If I were not sure that it is not so, I would have said that he was the Caliph, dressed in ragged clothes!"

"You are right, my friend," said Haroun Al Raschid, looking closer. "How remarkable to see one's likeness in the face of another."

"Let us put this money in his pocket, and let him wake to a day of prosperity," said Jaffer, and put a gold coin in the Caliph's hand.

The man lay snoring deeply as if he would never waken.

"I have a better idea," said Haroun, "let us take him to the palace, and let him sleep in my own bed tonight. We shall see what his history is, and try to help him further tomorrow."

So Jaffer and the Caliph between them gently lifted the sleeping man, and carried him to the palace. They took him to the Caliph's bed and, pulling off his old clothes, covered him with a silken bedspread.

No sooner had they done so, than there was a knock on the door.

Jaffer opened it, and there stood the Chief of the Army, General Harb.

"Is the Caliph awake?" asked the General. "There is very grave news from the battlefield. Our men are losing heart, and call for the Caliph to lead them!"

Haround Al Raschid spoke firmly, "I hear your words, General Harb. Wait for me but half an hour, I shall be ready to ride with you by then."

The Chief of the Army saluted and went away to order horses for himself and the Caliph.

"Jaffer," said Haroun, "I must go and fight under our banner until the Infidel is routed. Keep secret my departure, in case enemies hear of it and work mischief."

"But Your Highness, what about the beggar whom we have just brought in and put in your bed?" said the Vizier.

"He shall be told that he is the Caliph, and that he has not been well. Tell him anything, but keep him here, in my place, until I return." So saying, the Caliph put on his military cloak and took his sword from the wall. "I shall be back as soon as I can; in the meantime, Jaffer, my good friend, I rely on you to manage this deception as if my life depended upon it.

"May the blessings of Allah be upon you, noble Caliph," said the Vizier, "and send you victory!"

The Caliph put his finger to his lips and left the room by a hidden door.

Meanwhile, the man on the bed, whose name was Abdulla, awoke, and could not believe his own eyes.

Here he was, in a great room with costly hangings and carpets.

144

He saw that he was lying on a soft bed, covered with a silken bedspread. He sat up, with an aching head, wondering where he could possibly be.

Jaffer stood beside him, and bowed.

"What are your instructions, great Caliph?" he asked the wondering Abdulla. "You have not been well, and the doctor said that when you woke you would still feel weak. Command me, I am here to obey your slightest wish."

Abdulla stared at the Vizier and wondered if he had gone out of his mind. "Caliph? Caliph? I am not the Caliph," he said. "I have been looking for work all day long, and finding none, fell asleep, hungry and exhausted in the street. I have no money to take home to my wife and children, I cannot understand how it is that I..." He rubbed his head with one hand, and could not find any more words.

Soothingly, the Vizier told him that he was indeed the Caliph, that he had been ill, and if he wished to get up, his clothes would be brought. Abdulla, as if in a dream, rose from the bed, was dressed by a slave, and given a dish of the most delicious spiced rice. "If this is all in my imagination," he said to himself, "then who am I to dispute it? For it is a most pleasant dream, and I have no wish to wake."

So Abdulla reasoned, and began to enjoy his life. After a few days, he began to feel that he was the Caliph, and when the people sent petitions to him, he listened to them sympathetically. One poor woman said, in a letter which she gave to an official: "Mighty Haroun Al Raschid, my poor husband has not returned home after seven days, and I fear that something may have happened to him. I have no money with which to feed my children, send me, in Allah's Name, a sum so that I may carry on until he returns. He was looking for work, and may have wandered away somewhere in search of it. May Allah Bless and Keep Your Highness."

"Let this unfortunate creature be given a bag of gold," said Abdulla, handing the letter to Jaffer. "Somehow, her words strike me very forcibly. Here I am in this palace, with everything I need, and a woman like this is in such terrible straits! Go, attend to her case at once."

Now, the woman who had written the letter was Abdulla's own wife, and the reading of her letter distressed him. Somewhere in the back of his mind he felt he knew her story. "But," said he to himself, "if I am the Caliph, how can this be so? Or, if I am Abdulla dreaming that I am the Caliph, may I not dream that I could help my dear wife by sending her a bag of gold by the hand of the Vizier Jaffer?"

Abdulla's wife was delighted when the Court official brought her the gold, and she at once bought food and clothes for the family. As for her husband Abdulla, she almost hated him. "Has he not deserted us, in our need?" she said to her neighbours. "If it had not been for the goodness of the Caliph, we should have all been dead of hunger."

The real Caliph Haroun Al Raschid led his army to victory, and giving thanks to Allah, returned to Baghdad. He entered his own apartments by the hidden door, and as it was the dead of night, the false Caliph lay fast asleep in his bed. Silently, Haroun Al Raschid went to Jaffer's bedroom, and woke him.

"Victory is ours," said the Caliph. "Now I only want to sleep and sleep until this tiredness has left me."

"Your Highness," said the Vizier, "what shall we do then with the man whom the people thought to be you? He has done well in your absence, and thinks he is truly the Caliph!"

"He must go back to where we found him," said the weary Haroun Al Raschid, "put this tattered cloak around him and take him there." So the Vizier did as the Caliph commanded, and left Abdulla lying in the road where he had been on the night when this story began.

Abdulla awoke about dawn, and instead of his soft bed there was the hard road under him. "By Allah!" he cried, as the cocks roused him from sleep, "I knew that was a dream. As if I could have been the Caliph of Baghdad!"

In a pocket of his cloak there was a small bag, and he found a hundred gold pieces therein. He rubbed his head, and got to his feet. "I must go home at once," he thought. "Some Jinn must have left this here. I cannot understand what has happened to my torn old clothes! Here am I, in the street, with only an extremely tattered cloak and a bag of gold. Wait until my wife hears of this!"

He ran home as fast as he could and knocked on the door. Soon he heard the bolts being drawn, and a voice called: "Who is it?" The old servant put his head round the door.

As soon as he saw it was Abdulla, he cried, "Dear Master, so you are safe? My mistress gave you up for dead almost a week ago, and sent a petition to the Caliph!" Abdulla ran upstairs to his wife and showed her the bag of gold.

"Allah be praised!" she wept. "I thought you had deserted us, and all the time you were working to bring us such a lot of money! What did you do, to get it?"

Abdulla scratched his head. "I cannot really be sure, my dear," he said, "but I think I must have been carried away by a Jinn!"

The Miraculous Snake-Master of Agadir

In Morocco, there once lived a merchant called Abdul Salam, his wife and their daughter called Noora. When she was about seven years old, Noora's mother fell ill and died.

As Noora was an only child and she reminded Abdul Salam of his wife, he spoiled her in every possible way. He was always buying her pretty things and giving her all sorts of treats. The servants in the house grew tired of pandering to her whims and left her more and more to herself.

This continued until one night when thieves broke into the merchant's house and warehouse and stole everything that was of value. Since the servants absconded too, it was suspected that they had been in league with the thieves. Noora and her father found themselves quite alone in a virtually empty house.

He decided to go to the nearest big city, Agadir, to try to raise money from other merchants and begin afresh. Before he went, he asked the next door neighbours to look after Noora and gave them a little of the money he had left, to feed her till he returned. He could not take her because he had to walk to Agadir and it might take weeks to get together enough money to start again.

Noora felt very sad when her father left, for there was no-one to spoil her now. She went to the gate of the garden each day to look for his return, but in vain. For some weeks, the woman in the house next door fed her like her own children, but then she began to give her less and less. The other children taunted her with the fact that her father had left her there and bullied her generally. Noora took to crying herself to sleep at nights.

One day, she decided to run away and go to look for her father. She knew the road to the big city which he had taken and she thought if she just kept on walking she would get there eventually. Filling her pockets with nuts from the big walnut tree, she set off along the road in the early morning.

She walked and walked and the sun grew hotter and hotter. Blisters appeared on her feet and her mouth grew dry so she rested in the shade of a huge tree, taking off her sandals and munching a few of the walnuts.

Two ragged boys came towards her carrying a sack which had something wriggling about inside it. Laughing and shouting, and ignoring Noora altogether, they tied the sack onto one of the branches of the tree under which she sat. They gave the sack a few thumps with a stick and then ran off the way they had come.

Noora wondered what was in the sack, which was wriggling as if it were full of imps. But she was afraid to go near it and was just going to set off again when she heard a voice coming from inside the sack calling, "Please save me, save me from this sack and you shall be rewarded!"

Standing on tiptoe, she just managed to untie the sack and was surprised to find inside it, a large green and brown snake covered with lustrous scales. It had glittering black eyes and its long forked tongue flickered at her.

"Oh, are you going to bite me?" asked Noora starting back.

"No, no my child," said the snake, "I certainly will not. I promised to reward you if you released me and I shall keep my word. Say what it is that you most want and it shall be yours."

Noora immediately asked for a glass full of cold sherbet - and there it was in her right hand. She drank gratefully; then she thanked the snake and began to put on her sandals.

150

"Where are you going?" asked the snake, hanging from a branch just above her head in order to address her. The quick forked tongue flickered in and out of its mouth as it spoke but now she knew that it would not harm her, so she told her story.

"My father, Abdul Salam the merchant, has gone away to Agadir and I was getting very unhappy waiting for him. The village children are beginning to taunt me: they say he will never come back. So, I decided that I ought to go and look for him in Agadir."

"But did he not tell you to wait until he returned?" asked the snake. "You may miss him if he gets home before you."

Noora shook her head. "No, I would meet him here on the road: there is only one way to our house. I feel that something may have happened to my father and I must try to find him. Anyway, there is no food in the cupboard and the people next door are so unfriendly now that I have run away."

The snake looked at her out of its bright black beady eyes and said, "Let me hang round your neck and I will tell you where to go... my master will help you because you have saved my life." So, Noora put the snake around her neck and was surprised to find that it was smooth and sleek to the touch like a heavy silver necklace. She was not at all afraid of it and she covered the reptile up with her thin silk scarf. Then she started up the road towards Agadir much more cheerfully than before.

As she went along the dusty highway, the snake told her it was a creature possessed of the power to grant wishes for others but not for itself and that was why it could not free itself from the sack when the boys had caught it.

"I was lying sleeping innocently in the sun," said the snake, "when suddenly and without warning those two wretched boys came upon me and tied me up in a dirty old bag. I do not know what I would have done had you not been there to let me out." The snake went on: "I was glad that, because of my magical powers, I was able to get you a drink; now I see that you are growing tired - why do we not ride?"

Before Noora knew what was happening, she saw a beautiful little donkey-cart appear in the roadway and a small black boy in

151

a red coat, green boots and a silver ring in his right ear was helping her into the cart. The snake said "Take us to the house of my master and hasten, for this young lady must find her father!" and off they went as fast as the long-eared donkey could go.

In no time at all, the cart stopped at a huge white-walled house, set among tall whispering palm trees, which gave shade along a wide avenue. Noora was beginning to feel nervous, for she had never been away from her own village before, but the snake, which was still looped around her neck, said "Do not distress yourself, dear child. My master will help you to find your father."

"But... but... who is he? This big house must belong to a very important man."

"Yes," replied the snake, "he is none other than the Grand Snake-Master of Agadir. He is Lord of all the snakes of Morocco and there are vast numbers of us, all under his command."

The small black boy in the red coat helped Noora down off the cart. She pulled her veil over her head and straightened her many-coloured skirts; then she went after the young fellow through a great archway into a beautiful shady courtyard, where there were potted plants and comfortable chairs of carved wood amid the sweetly splashing fountains, which kept the air fresh and cool.

"Sit here for a short while and rest," said the snake, slipping from Noora's neck onto the marble mosaic steps leading to a large wooden door. "I will pay my respects to my master and tell him that you need his help. He will no doubt want to thank you for your good deed."

As the snake glided away, Noora saw that fruit and a glass of pure refreshing water had appeared on the small circular table beside her chair. She ate and drank, feeling as if she were in Paradise. Or could it be a dream? She rubbed her eyes and pinched herself but the shady courtyard and the tall whispering palm trees did not fade. About her, cooling fountains tinkled into huge marble basins in which there were gleaming golden carp swimming languidly.

A little time later, the great wooden door swung open and

Noora saw the snake with shiny green and brown scales gliding towards her. Behind it walked the tallest, thinnest man she had ever seen. His eyes were a bright glittering blue, his hair as white as the snow upon the Atlas Mountains and he was dressed in a long robe of dark blue cotton. On his head was a red fez, decorated with a strip of cobra snakeskin. On his feet were yellow shoes and he walked with a gliding motion, just like a snake.

Noora jumped up but found that she could not speak: she was completely tongue-tied. However, the tall man smiled and soon put her at her ease. He sat in a chair beside her and motioned her to sit. A drink of lime juice appeared in his right hand and another on the table by her side. The snake coiled itself around one of the legs of its master's chair, its tongue flickering.

"You have done me a great service," he said, "by saving the life of my beloved snake, which was tied up in a sack by those unfeeling children. Do they not realise that snakes are Allah's creatures, just as we are? I thank you very much for your help and if there is anything I can do to repay you, then you only have to ask."

Noora's nervousness vanished as she spoke to the Snake-Master, for she knew that he was a powerful magician and would help her to find her father. She told him her troubles from beginning to end. When she had finished, the old Snake-Master said, "I will send all my snakes to every place in Agadir where merchants gather. By tomorrow morning at the latest, one of them will have found your good father. Now, the snake here will take you to my wife's part of the house, where you may bathe and rest until the evening meal."

He got up and, before Noora could thank him, had disappeared as silently as he had come before her. Gliding in front of her, the snake took Noora to a room where a fat lady in a white caftan sewn with pearls was boxing the ears of her maids and scolding them. Noora was apprehensive when she saw her but then the Snake-Master's wife smiled and made her welcome. Soon she was quite at ease and was being bathed and dressed in clean cool cotton garments, far more suitable for a feast in that huge white

153

house than the dusty clothes she had been wearing.

The snakes went all over the city of Agadir, creeping in and out of holes in walls and looking through windows and gliding swiftly along balconies, until they found where Noora's father was that very night.

The Snake-Master had Noora brought to him just before she went to bed (on a comfortable couch in the bedroom of his eldest daughter) and said, "My child, my snakes have reported that your father is in such-and-such a caravanserai, where travellers and merchants and pilgrims to Mecca congregate, but he is ill of a fever and so I have sent a doctor to him."

Noora gave a cry and burst into tears but the Snake-Master went on, "Do not worry, all will be well with your father by tomorrow. I have made arrangements so that he and you will return to your own home as soon as he can travel. He has been told that you are safe and well here in my house and he is glad. Tomorrow then, you shall see your father. Goodnight and sleep peacefully."

Noora longed to go to her father at once, yet she knew it would be better to wait until the morrow. As soon as the cock crowed, she was up sitting in the beautiful garden and watching the sun rise in all its glory.

As she watched, a long line of camels passed the house with the white walls, their bells tinkling and huge bundles of merchandise fastened in bulging panniers to their sides. The snake with shiny green and brown scales came gliding towards Noora and said, "My master has sent these loads to your father, so that he may now be able to start trading again. By the time the bales of cloth, dried fruits, precious stones and other merchandise arrive at your village, you and your father will have caught up with the camel-train on riding camels and can accompany it back to your house. Thanks to your kindness, prosperity will be with your father again, so remember that one good turn deserves another!"

Noora ran to find and thank the fat lady whose caftan was covered with pearls and to say goodbye; but she could not find the tall, thin, generous Snake-Master. She begged the snake which she had rescued to thank the Master very much indeed for finding her father and for the marvellous caravan of merchandise.

As promised, her father came soon afterwards, and though he was cross with Noora for leaving home to follow him, he forgave her in the joy of seeing her again.

With the help of the Snake-Master's caravan, he was able to set up his trading establishment once more and become wealthy again.

But strangely enough, though Abdul Salam often went along the road to Agadir and tried to find the white-walled house of the Snake-Master to thank him and return the camels and repay the cost of the goods which they had carried on their backs; he could never find it again. It had simply vanished from sight.

I wonder where it had gone? Maybe it was there all the time, but the Snake-Master of Agadir did not want to be thanked - so glad was he to have one of his precious and beloved snakes returned to him - so he made his home invisible to Abdul Salam the Merchant.

And it is a strange fact that in all her long life, Noora was never ever bitten by a snake.

Prince Adil And The Lions

Long ago and far away, there lived a King who had a handsome son of whom he was very fond and who resembled his father Azad as he had been in his youth.

One day, King Azad said to his Grand Vizier, "Come, let us take my son to the Cave of the Lion and tell him what is expected of him, now he is eighteen years old."

They went together to Adil and the Grand Vizier said, "Your Highness, it has always been the custom in this noble family, when the heir to the throne is of the age you are now, that he should be given a certain test. This is to establish beyond question whether he is fit to be the future ruler of our people or not. Come with us now and we will show you where you are to be tested."

The Prince followed his father and the courtier to a large door set in the wall of a rocky cave and studded with nails. There was a grille in the door, through which could be heard the roaring of a lion.

"See here, my son," said the King stroking his beard, "inside is a huge forest-bred lion, which it will be your duty to wrestle with and subdue with dagger and sword - choose when you wish to do so. Every male in our family who is in direct line to the throne has had to pass this test."

The Prince looked through the grille and paled, for he saw a very large lion indeed pacing up and down a cavernous den, which was littered with bones. The animal had a shaggy mane and extremely sharp white teeth, which were bared in a bad-tempered snarl. Every now and again it gave another terrifying roar.

"Wrestle? Subdue? Kill that?" stammered the youth. "How am I to do that? I have never done more than kill a deer or set my hawk after another bird. I really think that a lion of that size and strength is beyond me."

"Have no fear," interposed the Grand Vizier. "You need not do it now. Some time in the future will do, when you get used to the idea. By Allah's Grace, you will get the confidence you need when you have thought it over for a bit. All your forebears did so, eventually."

The King smiled and signalled to a slave to throw some meat to the animal. Its roars turned to contented growls as it tore the food to pieces.

For days afterwards, though the King treated his son as kindly as before, Adil had a feeling that this task was hanging over him and his father was anxious for him to kill the lion at once. He could not take pleasure in the normal joys of life, thinking of the contest. All the sparkle had gone out of his existence for he felt that he was expected to go into the lion's den and emulate the doings of the famous heroes of legend, when he did not feel in the least like one.

One night, after tossing and turning sleeplessly in his room, he got up and dressed. Then, filling his moneybelt with a sufficient number of gold coins, he went in the bright moonlight to the royal stables. There he found a sleeping groom and got him to saddle his own favourite steed. He told the groom to tell the King, his father, that he had gone on a journey.

Without a backward glance, he rode away, seeking the answer to his problem. By morning, he had come upon a pleasant river, with beautiful meadows on either side. Here he dismounted to let his horse have a much needed drink. Presently he heard the sound of a flute being played and saw a young shepherd leading a flock of sheep to pasture. Adil asked him if there was somewhere nearby where he might stay for a few days. The shepherd said that he would take him to his master, a rich man who lived in a big house close by.

There, the owner of the house and surrounding lands invited Adil to dine with him. "From whence do you come and what is the state of your crops?" asked the older man, who was called Haroun. The prince replied evasively saying, "I have troubles at home which have caused me to leave, so I will ask you to let me say no more than this for the time being: I am seeking an answer to some personal problems."

The older man immediately replied that the prince should stay as a guest as long as he felt the need and should treat the house as his own home. The Prince's horse was led away and stabled with Haroun's own and Adil thought he would like to stay for a long time in these tranquil surroundings.

Each day he discovered some new enchanting spot, where could be heard the sound of flutes from every shepherd in the area. There were indeed a great number, for this was The Land of The Heavenly Flute-Players.

But one night to his horror, he heard the roaring of lions not far away from the house and at breakfast he mentioned the matter.

"Oh yes," responded Haroun calmly. "This place is infested with wild lions; they hunt all night and for most of the year. I am surprised that you have not heard them before. It is the reason for the high wall around my garden. Else they would be carrying away the members of my family!" and he laughed uproariously, as if at some hearty joke.

The prince's heart was filled with fear. As soon as he could get his horse ready for travel, he bade farewell to the hospitable Haroun and rode off once more as fast as his horse could carry him. He journeyed on and on and soon the green valleys and groves were left behind and the country became more barren. The road disappeared in a hard, sandy plain and there was not one blade of green grass for as far as the eye could see.

Now and again the wind stirred the dust from some low sand dunes which, piled like drifts of snow, made the scenery seem even more desolate. The sun blazed down and Arab thoroughbred though his horse was, it slowed considerably and began to falter, stumbling often. Adil knew that he had to find water for both of them and soon. Silently he prayed that over the next dune there might be an encampment of Bedouin or a small oasis.

As if in answer to his prayer, there was a line of black tents! As he drew near, several mounted warriors approached, flourishing their guns, and hailed him with cries of "Asalaamawaliekum," and shouts of "People and safety!"

They escorted him to their leader, the Sheikh, who bade him welcome, saying that he was now their honoured guest and should stay with them as long as he wished.

After a wonderful meal of boiled mutton, spiced rice and figs and dates of incredible sweetness, the Sheikh asked Adil what chance had brought him in that direction.

"Please ask me no more," said the prince. "Suffice it to say that I am one who has left home with a problem, which I hope to resolve by absenting myself from my father's country for the time being until I am surer of my situation."

The Sheikh inclined his head, stroked his beard and took another puff at his water-pipe. "Time gives us all the answers," he murmured, "if we can be patient."

Next day, he asked the young man to come hunting antelope with him and the day after that to go hawking, which Adil enjoyed very much. As he breathed the fine fresh desert air and ate the ample meals provided by the Sheikh and his household, the prince felt he could remain here under the stars and in the golden sunlight for ever.

But one day, when he had enjoyed the Bedouin's hospitality for two happy weeks, the old Sheikh said, "My son, the people here, living in these tents under my protection, are pleased with you, as I am, and admire the spirit with which you have joined us in our simple sports. But these men and I myself are all seasoned warriors who frequently have to wage war upon other tribes.

160

Then great personal bravery is necessary for the survival of our own tribe. Therefore, my men and I would like you to undertake a test so that we could see some evidence of your prowess. Two miles to the south of this area is a low range of hills infested with lions. Rise then early tomorrow and, after the Prayer of the Dawn, take the finest of our valiant steeds and with sword and spear, kill one of those wild creatures. When you have done that and brought us the skin, then you will have proved yourself in our eyes, my dear young friend."

Prince Adil's face paled beneath his tan as fear gripped him and as he wished the Sheikh goodnight he knew he could not face those savage creatures.

"Good heavens," he thought as he slipped away from the evening meal, seeing all those happy tribal faces shining in the light of the cooking fires, "it seems to be my bad luck to find lions wherever I go. I cannot understand it... why did I leave home if not to avoid them?"

When everyone was asleep, he crept out of his tent, found his horse and silently left the place where he had been so happy for two long weeks. Was it to be his fate to travel the world forever without finding any place where there were no lions?

He rode on and on into the starry night. Then, as the rosy fingers of dawn began to show in the sky, he saw a charming region of hill and dale covered with wild flowers and his horse drank from a tranquil pool. Then, in the fast-brightening light of day, he saw a wonderful palace, finer than any he had known. It was of rose-coloured stone with pillars of lapis lazuli and balconies of carved painted wood. There were fountains in the gardens all around the palace, singing birds in flowering trees and many pavilions in the gardens, covered with jasmine and sweet-scented roses.

"Truly, this is a veritable Paradise on Earth!" said Adil to himself as he approached the palace. At the great gate, guards led him to an inner courtyard and a boy took his horse to be rubbed down and fed. Adil was taken to a guest chamber where he could wash and change into fresh clothes, laid out by smiling servants.

At last, he was brought before the Emir, a grey-bearded man of

161

much charm and wealth who, amid the usual pleasantries, asked him what had brought him in that direction. The Princess Peri-Zade, his daughter, was having breakfast with her father and Adil was delighted at her beauty and grace as she poured him a drink of sweet sherbet from a crystal jug. The Princess had wonderful almond eyes and a perfect complexion with hair, black as a raven's wing, plaited into many small strands.

"My situation is such that I... I... cannot talk about it," stammered the enraptured Prince Adil, trying not to look at the lovely Peri-Zade with whom he had immediately fallen in love. "Suffice it to say that I have had to leave my own country because I have to solve a problem..." he said and then fell silent, sipping the delicious sherbet with lowered eyes.

The Emir nodded wisely and stroked his beard. "I understand," he replied quietly and then began speaking of other matters. The Princess began to look at Adil from under her long lashes, thinking that he was a very good-looking young man. She wondered what his problem might be and if she could help him with it.

After the meal, the Emir showed Adil around the Palace. If the exterior was grand, how much more extravagant was the inside. Steps of polished marble and red porphyry led to various rooms which were each furnished in woods from every part of the world. The walls and ceilings were covered with turquoise and gold mosaics, frescoes and mirrors.

Bowls of precious stones and rose-pink shells were displayed on tables of carved jade. The windows were of translucent glass and were stained in delightful colours, some as pink as the sunrise, others as green as the depths of the sea. When the rays of the sun shone through, the tessellated floors were lit with wonderful colours. Underfoot in the great durbar room, the carpets were as soft as silk; some had trees sewn with gold fruits, others had animals and birds so cunningly wrought that Adil was astonished that they had been made by human hands.

The Emir led Adil to the best guest chamber, where he begged him to change into the fresh clothes on the bed and invited him to stay as long as it was possible for him to remain.

Left to himself, looking at the splendour all around him and dressed in his richly-embroidered garments, Adil thought that this would be the one place where he could remain for the rest of his life.

Several days passed; and the Princess Peri-Zade delighted in showing Adil the garden at different hours of the day. One evening, strolling along the jasmine-scented paths, he listened to her singing a song for him and accompanying herself on the lute; an instrument which she played with great skill. The Palace was lit from top to bottom with thousands of candles. Slaves hurried hither and thither preparing delicacies for the evening feast.

Suddenly Adil heard a sound, which made the hairs rise on the back of his neck. "Stop!" he cried to the Princess. "What was that?"

"What was what?" she asked rather crossly, as she was annoyed at his apparent lack of interest in her music. "I heard nothing; surely it was your imagination." She went on playing and then Adil heard the sound again.

"Stop at once please, dear Princess," he said urgently. "It was over there, in the bushes... it sounded... it sounded like a lion!"

She laughed and made a face at him. "That is only Rustum, our Watchman as we call him!" She smiled, "He is the pet of the whole court and at this time of night, he patrols the Palace grounds. I have known him since he was a tiny cub; he sleeps just outside my room!"

Prince Adil went pale and suggested that, as the night was growing cold, they should return to the Palace. At the feast later Adil, seated to the right of the Emir, could scarcely eat for thinking of when he would have to face the lion, who was now roaring quite loudly in the garden. No-one else seemed to notice the noise and all but he were enjoying the excellent meal.

At the end of the feast, his host rose and took Adil to the top of the marble stairs which led to the guest chamber. There, at the top, stood the huge and ferocious-looking lion. Adil would have turned and gone in the opposite direction had not the Emir said, "Look, you are much honoured, my son; good old Rustum is waiting to take you to your bedroom! He doesn't do that for

163

many who come here, I can tell you. He only gets annoyed if he thinks anyone fears him," the Emir laughed, "but he is really extremely tame."

"I fear him," whispered the Prince, "I really do..." but the Emir did not appear to hear. He bade his guest goodnight and the lion padded beside Adil as he made his way to his own door. Getting to his room, the young man managed to enter quickly and close the door.

The lion waited outside and it seemed to Adil that all night long he snuffled at the lock and tried to turn the handle with his teeth or paws. In the morning, Adil got up after a very disturbed night and opened the door. The lion was gone.

Then and there, Adil made up his mind to return home. There were so many lions in the world that it would be better to fight the lion in the cave and get it over with, than to keep running all his life.

As soon as he was washed and dressed, he went to the Potentate and told him, "O Great Emir, I ask permission to leave your Palace now and fight my own problem in my own way, or I know I will never be at peace with myself. I am a coward and I want to change that for my father's sake. I am the son of King Azad and I fled from a duty which all the sons of our family have to perform. I am ashamed and know that I can never ask for the hand of a lady like the Princess Peri-Zade if I do not face my Kismet and fight the lion in the cave."

"Well spoken, my son," said the Emir. "I knew who you were when first you came for you closely resemble your father as a young man and I have always respected and admired King Azad. Go, fight the lion and I will give you my daughter, Peri-Zade, for she has already spoken of you to me with affection." He smiled then and laid his hand affectionately on Adil's shoulder.

The Prince mounted his horse and galloped off till he came to the encampment of black tents, where he had spent such a happy time not long before. The Bedouin Sheikh was sitting smoking his water-pipe when Adil rode up, and saluted the young man kindly.

"Welcome, Prince Adil," said he, "I knew your dear father

well when we were both about your age... in fact, you look more like him now than ever: though I noticed the resemblance before, which was how I guessed who you were."

Then Adil told him that he was on his way home to fight the lion in the cave. The Sheikh was delighted and asked him to spend the night with him so as to be ready to start at dawn the following day.

Well rested, Adil rode away at dawn towards his own country. Suddenly he found that he was longing to see his home again, lion and all. He could scarcely wait to tell his father that he was ready to face the great creature in the cave.

In a while, he arrived in the beautiful country of the Heavenly Flute-Players. To his delight, he saw the same boy as before, urging his sheep along to the tunes of the flute. Later the owner of the flocks came out of his shady courtyard to greet the Prince. After taking some refreshment, Adil explained he could not stay as he was on his way back to his father's palace. "For," he explained, "when I came here before I was nothing but a coward who wanted to escape his fate. Now I am ready to take on the lion. Whatever the outcome, each of my forebears has had to fight such a one; I will place my trust in Allah the Compassionate."

"So be it," responded the old man. "I am glad indeed to hear that you have come to terms with your problem. I knew that you (being the true son of your royal father - who was once my boon companion when we studied together) would in time face up to your responsibilities. Go, and Allah be with you!"

After saying farewell, Adil was once more on his way and in due course arrived in his own country. "Lead me at once to the cave of that ferocious lion with which I must wrestle, for I feel strong enough now to attempt the fight!" he said boldly to the Grand Vizier, after kissing his father's hands in salutation.

The old king embraced the young Prince with many expressions of joy and, together with the Grand Vizier, the three made their way once more to the lion's den.

The sword and dagger Adil carried shone brightly in the sun. Then, as a slave opened the huge door to the cave, Adil went bravely into the gloomy den. The lion began to roar, crouching down with lashing tail. Then rising up, it came at the Prince, its huge jaws agape.

The Prince gazed at the beast fearlessly, weapons in hand, while the King, the Grand Vizier and the slave looked on silently. The lion gave another roar, louder than before, and charged towards him. Then, to Adil's astonishment, the monster began to rub its head against his knees and licked his boots like a pet dog!

The Grand Vizier now called out, "Oh auspicious Prince, you now see that this lion is as tame as any devoted slave and would injure no-one. You have passed the test by going into the den. Proof of your valour is complete; you are now worthy to be our future king, Allah be praised!"

The young man could scarcely believe what had happened and when he left the cave, the lion followed him like an affectionate friend, gambolling beside him till it was returned to its den by the slave. The King congratulated his son on his courage, which now was never to be doubted. Adil was, by Allah's Grace, fit and worthy to be King after him.

There was much rejoicing in the Palace. Next day, there was also much festivity in every home in the surrounding town as, following tradition, many gold and silver coins were thrown by the delighted King to the crowds who collected in the great courtyard below the royal balcony.

Adil told his father that he had asked the father of the beautiful Peri-Zade for her hand, if King Azad would give his blessing to the match. The King agreed and a fast-riding messenger was despatched to the faraway country where she lived.

To Adil, it seemed an eternity before the cavalcade bringing his beloved to him, arrived. She came attended by a concourse of her relatives and friends, all of them dressed in the finest wedding clothes. The sight of the Princess Peri-Zade, riding a pure white Arab mare into the great courtyard of his palace, clad in the finest silk and arrayed with costly jewels, remained in Prince Adil's memory to the end of his days.

The wedding festivities went on for seven days and nights and there was not one tear in any eye in the whole of that happy

166

kingdom for the entire duration of the wedding feast.

So, they lived happily ever after and, when Adil became King after his father, he had inscribed on the floor of his private study - in letters of gold - the words "Never run away from a lion."

The Keeper Of The King's Horses

Once upon a time, many ages ago, there lived a powerful and arrogant king. He was the owner of many palaces, and ships carried rich merchandise from far-away lands to supply him with all the treasures of the then-known world. Hundreds of beautiful mares and stallions of the finest Arabian stock were kept in his stables. His mighty army was greatly feared by his enemies, and his justice was known to be swift by all wrong-doers in every corner of his domain.

Those were the days of bows and arrows, and when he went hunting, even with other Kings or Princes, Sultans or Caliphs, his weapons were always the finest of all.

One day, to rest from the affairs of State, and the ostentatious ceremonies of the Court, where ambassadors of many countries came daily to pay him homage, he went off hunting - alone. Further and further into the depths of the forest he went, without any companion nor even a page to carry his arrows. He was only thinking of the chase and his mind was at peace. Once or twice he had sighted a fine golden hind, but each time he fitted an arrow to the bow, she moved into the undergrowth and disappeared from sight. Even as he glimpsed her again she vanished, protected once more by her natural colouring which matched that of the forest.

Fuming at his ill fortune in losing his quarry yet again, the king threw himself down at the foot of an ancient tree, which, by the girth of its trunk, must have been at least two hundred years old. A few moments later, he was startled by the sharp sound of the breaking of a twig underfoot and saw an old man standing within a few feet of him.

Fearing that, despite his years, this was either a robber or an assassin, the royal hunter fitted an arrow to his bow again and shouted: "Who are you and what are you doing here? Come a step nearer and you will be a dead man!"

The aged one knelt and with guileless eyes, looked the king boldly in the face saying, "Live for ever, O King! Allah's Peace be upon you, your auspicious Majesty; You have two hundred mares and stallions in the royal stables and I know the name of every one, for I am Hamid, the keeper of your Majesty's horses. Yet you recognise a hind in the forest more readily than the face of one of your true subjects!"

Then the monarch felt deep shame in his heart. Raising the brave old man up, he asked his forgiveness.

Together, they returned to the Palace; the contrite king conversing freely with Hamid, the Keeper of the King's Horses who had spent fifty years in the stables.

The once-proud ruler resolved to get to know his subjects better and from that day on, he took every opportunity to make friends with them. For he realised then that it was a part of his responsibilities to know each one of his subjects as well as the old man knew his horses. And Allah sent him many years of peace from that day onwards.

The Young Sultan And
The Dream Angel

Once upon a time there was a Sultan who had seven daughters, but no son. The princesses were all very beautiful, but the Sultan felt that his heart's desire had been denied him. He wanted a son more than anything else in the whole world.

After he had given thousands of gold coins to the poor, and built a great mosque to the Glory of Allah with a dozen minarets set with turquoise and pearls, the Sultana one day presented him with a fine young son.

The young prince, Ahmad, was spoiled by his father, his mother, his seven sisters and all the courtiers. Consequently, he grew up to become a good-looking but very tiresome young man, with no idea of the value of money.

After his father died, young Sultan Ahmad began to spend the fortune the old Sultan had accumulated. He bought rich clothes, fine horses, racing camels and jewels as big as pigeon's eggs. In vain did his mother, the Sultana, try to stop him; in vain did the seven sisters insist that they should be given some of their father's money to have for dowries when they were to be given in marriage. The heartless Ahmad turned a deaf ear to all their

171

pleas - and to the advice of his Viziers. He continued to spend and spend on one luxury after another, leaving his Viziers to run the country.

One night, after a particularly rich dinner on the finest delicacies in the land, he had a strange dream.

A beautiful angel appeared in his bedroom and spoke to him: "No joy so great but it cometh to an end! Get thee to the City of Damascus far away in the West. There you shall find an old man called Ramadan. He will help you to marry a King's daughter. But who is to help you to curb this dreadful affliction of yours - your heedlessness with money ?"

The angel shook his head as if in thought and then added, "If you do not heed my words, you will rue it."

"Who are you?" asked Ahmad faintly. "Are you good or evil?"

"I am all Goodness," said the apparition. "I am your Dream Angel, your Heavenly Protector."

Ahmad woke, extremely puzzled. However, he knew he was becoming very unpopular with his people because of his wild spending. And he was very intrigued by the Dream Angel's mention of the King's daughter whom he would marry. None of the neighbouring princesses had ever shown the least interest in him: his mother, the Dowager Sultana, told him that it was on account of his spendthrift habits.

He decided he would go to Damascus as the Angel had directed. At the least, it was a challenge to go and find the old man called Ramadan.

He dressed quietly and sensibly for once, in a manner suitable for a long journey to the West. He bade farewell to his mother and sisters and rode off, saying he was going to travel incognito throughout the country.

After many days, he arrived in Damascus. Sitting in a coffee-house, he asked the owner casually if he knew of an old man called Ramadan and where he might be found.

Luckily, the coffee-house owner did. He directed Ahmad to Ramadan's house which was quite near to the hostelry where Ahmad had found comfortable lodging for himself and his horse. He knocked at an old brass-studded wooden door and it was

172

Ramadan himself who opened it.

"I am Ahmad," said the young Sultan. "In a dream, an angel told me that I should travel to Damascus to see you. I have ridden a long way and am very tired. May I come in?"

"Of course. Please enter, most auspicious Sultan," said Ramadan. "You are the very image of your late father, (may Allah accept his soul into Paradise!) and I bid you welcome, for his sake. Also I have been expecting you!"

Ahmad sat down on a divan, and asked: "Tell me why I have to come here? There must be some reason that I have been able to find you so easily. It seems as though Kismet itself guided me."

Ramadan explained: "When you were born, there was a mystical prophecy made by the Seven Good Jinn who attended your father, the Sultan, at the birth."

"What prophecy?" asked Ahmad. "And what connection is there between my family and the Jinn?"

"Your father was a friend of the Lord of Magicians and Master of the Jinn, King Suliman, Son of David (upon whom be peace!). King Suliman has decreed that a beautiful princess - imprisoned in a tower by her father as a punishment for her disobedience - should be rescued by stealth and immediately brought to him, as he has fallen in love with her," replied Ramadan.

"But how do I come into this, and what is the mystical prophecy?" inquired Ahmad.

"At your birth it was prophesied that it would fall to you to perform a task for King Suliman, Son of David (upon whom be peace). Now it so happens that the beautiful princess Ayesha can only be rescued by a Sultan, one who is young and comely. She has already refused to go to King Suliman (upon whom be peace!) because he is so much older than she is."

"But how can I possibly find her and the tower?" asked Ahmad, "I haven't any idea where they are or how to rescue her."

"Here is a magic mirror into which you may look for guidance," said Ramadan. "It will help you on your way."

"What will happen after I find the Princess and take her to

173

King Suliman?" Ahmad wanted to know.

"There is no end to what the Lord of All Magicians, Master of Enchanted Beings and Beasts may do for you as a reward for performing this task," said the old man. "You can ask for anything you desire, once you have freed the Princess from the tower and taken her with all speed to the Palace of King Suliman, Son of David (upon whom be peace!)."

"I will ride at dawn," agreed Ahmad, "as soon as I can get my horse from the stables. He needs a rest, as do I, if we are to make an early start."

That night, the Princess in her tower also dreamed that an angel appeared at the foot of her bed. He told her not to fear - a handsome young Sultan would soon come to rescue her. He would throw a silken ladder up to her balcony, and she was to climb down it with perfect trust.

"He will not carry me off to that old King Suliman, will he?" the Princess wanted to know, "I have already refused him but my father wants to make me marry him. He has imprisoned me in this tower until I agree! But he is so old, he must be about a hundred!" she wailed.

"No, he is much older than a hundred years," said the Dream Angel, "that I can tell you - nobody knows just how old he is. But you will have to go to his Palace so that the young Sultan Ahmad may plead on your behalf with King Suliman, Son of David (upon whom be peace!)." With that, the vision vanished and the Princess was left to weep and lament alone.

In the morning, booted and spurred, the young Sultan set off with the mirror in his hand and followed the road he saw therein. Now and again, the face of the Princess Ayesha appeared: alone in her room at the top of the tower where she had been imprisoned by her father. Each time, tears were trembling on her eyelashes and the corners of her mouth were turned down in sadness. When he had seen her three times, Ahmad had fallen deeply in love with her and was determined to have her for himself despite the decree of the Great Lord of Magicians, King Suliman and his desire to marry her himself!

Ahmad's horse covered the miles very swiftly and soon he

174

brought his master to the foot of the tall white tower where the Princess Ayesha was confined. There, leaning over the balcony, was the unfortunate Princess.

Ahmad called up to her softly saying, "I am Ahmad, come to rescue you! Quick, here is a silken ladder for you to climb down. Catch it and fasten it securely."

The Princess did as she was bid, knowing that her dream had come true. Soon she would be out of the tower where she had been imprisoned for so long. In moments she had fastened the strong silken ladder to the iron balcony and climbed down as lightly as any monkey, for she was very nimble.

As they looked at one another, the sun shone brightly and the Princess's eyes filled with joy. She laughed up at Ahmad as if she had known him all her life: "Thank you, O Sultan, thank you so much for saving me," she cried. And both were hoping that they could spend the rest of their days together.

Then Sultan Ahmad looked into the magic mirror and saw old Ramadan pointing up the road to where, in the far distance, a magnificent palace reared up into the clouds. It was the palace of King Suliman, Son of David and now he must go with the Princess Ayesha and face the ancient King of Magicians - to beg for her liberty so that she could become his wife.

With the Princess Ayesha perched on the saddle in front of Ahmad, they set off at a steady pace and he said, "I can never part with you now, dearest Princess, but we must go to the Palace of him who controls the movements of the Jinn and is the most powerful Lord of Magical Beings, both in this land and in the Land of Enchantment. If we were not to go to him and explain that we are in love, he would never let us live in peace together. His wrath would follow us to the ends of the Earth!"

"Perhaps he will turn us into strange creatures, toads, or... or... maybe monsters!" whispered Ayesha, her eyes wide with fear. "Oh, do we have to go to him? Will he really understand and forgive?"

"We will have to try to persuade him and trust in Allah," replied Ahmad and they spoke no more. Following the way shown by the magic mirror, they arrived at the huge gates of the

175

palace of King Suliman, the golden towers of which rose high into the clouds.

There were no guards or servants to be seen as the horse cantered up to the gates. They opened as if by invisible hands, and closed behind them in the same silent manner.

Ahmad and Ayesha dismounted and left the horse in the courtyard, tied to a railing. A huge golden door, carved with strange magical talismans, opened as Ahmad lifted his hand to knock and they went forward cautiously, hand in hand. They found themselves in a lofty hall, brightly lit with a thousand candles.

Suddenly a loud voice, coming as if from a cabinet in the middle of the room, startled them. "Welcome to my Palace of the Winds. Rest here, eat and drink, and I will be with you presently." Immediately a table was placed before them by invisible hands, and the rarest of food and drink was served. Sweet music came, it seemed, from the walls of the magnificent hall and put them at their ease. Chairs of gold and carved wood appeared and soon Ahmad and Ayesha were seated, eating and drinking their fill. When they could eat no more, the table vanished as it had come. Though Ahmad and Ayesha had eyes only for each other, they could not but be aware of the wonderful carpets underfoot, the embroidered tapestries and rare hangings on the walls, all richly illuminated by huge candelabra.

Suddenly, the music stopped and the painted lacquer cabinet in the middle of the hall opened. King Suliman, Son of David, King of all Magicians stepped out. He was a tall, commanding figure, with a white beard and turban embroidered with silver stars. His robe was of shining green satin on which a belt of opals glowed. His boots were of finest leather, and on his fingers rare jewels shone in the candlelight.

The most hypnotic eyes the young people had ever seen held them with a strange compulsion: they felt sure that he could tell what they were thinking. Both bowed low before him.

"Greetings, great Suliman, may peace be upon you!" said Sultan Ahmad bravely, while Princess Ayesha covered her face with her veil and stood swaying in fear beside him.

"And upon you too, be peace," responded the Lord of all

Magicians kindly: "I am glad you have come here. I was watching you in my magical opal stone, here in the ring on my right hand. But you have something to tell me, have you not? Well, out with it!" His remarkable eyes fell upon Ahmad and held his gaze.

Ahmad replied, "Because my father (may his soul rest in Paradise) was a friend of Your Majesty's, I was happy to carry out this task which you had decreed." His voice faltered, "But... but now we have fallen in love with each other, and we beg you to let us go away together. The Princess is very sorry that she has refused Your Majesty's offer, but she cannot now refuse the demands of our two hearts!"

"Bravely said," smiled the Great King of Magicians, "I knew this as I know all things which concern me, so, for the sake of your dear father I will allow you to carry this beautiful creature away to be your wife. May you be happy together until your lives end!"

"As Allah wills!" murmured Ahmad faintly, "I thank you from the bottom of my heart, most Magnanimous Ruler."

Then, plucking up courage, he continued, "There is one further boon I would crave from you. Please - could you place upon me, a spell to curb my spending habits, which I know now to be a weakness and a curse?"

"Very well," said King Suliman, "I will give you that as a wedding present. From this day forward you will have a true knowledge of the value of money and will spend only in a proper and a prudent manner."

As the happy lovers thanked him with great joy, and many compliments, the great King of Magicians raised his hands, and all became darkness within that huge hall. The candles were blown out as if by a mighty blast of air and the voice of Suliman wished them farewell. Clutching at each other, Ahmad and Ayesha felt themselves swept up, up, up into the air and everything went black for them.

When they opened their eyes, they were once more on their horse's back, riding along the road they had come. The sun was shining, and behind them the pointed golden towers of King

177

Suliman's palace reached up into the clouds.

"What miracles we have seen!" Ahmad cried. "Did they indeed happen, my love? Let us now ride as fast as we can until we reach my kingdom, so that the preparations for our wedding may commence, dearest Ayesha."

"Yes," she replied. "It has been a day of miracles... my escape from that horrible tower, the love which has come to us, and the many kindnesses of King Suliman (upon whom be peace!) - to me in releasing me to go with you... *and* to you by his spell to give you the knowledge to handle money properly!"

"Time will tell if that really has happened," laughed Ahmad, as he held her tightly in his left arm, his right grasping the horse's reins.

After many days journey, they arrived at last in Sultan Ahmad's own country. The Dowager Sultana and the seven sisters wept for joy when they saw their brother safely home at last. When the Sultana saw the beautiful Princess Ayesha, she was delighted at the prospect of having such a lovely daughter-in-law. She immediately put at her disposal a fine private apartment in the Harem until the wedding could be arranged.

Meanwhile, the Royal Treasurer approached Sultan Ahmad as soon as he had rested from the journey and said, "Your Majesty, the camel-loads of gold which arrived today have been accommodated in the bullion-vaults. May I say on behalf of the officials of your Treasury how delighted we all are that your coffers are now full again, after the anxieties over the depletion of the treasure left by the late Sultan." He coughed delicately.

"Camel-loads of gold?" repeated Ahmad. "Arrived today?" Though overjoyed, he was completely mystified by this news. From where could the gold have come?

The Royal Treasurer handed him a scroll, tied with a green ribbon. Ahmad undid the ribbon, and read: "Your treasury has been replenished by Order of the Great Suliman, Son of David. Do not waste these gifts, which should last you the rest of your days, if Allah wills!" The letter was sealed with red wax, on which was the imprint of Suliman's Seal, known throughout the Arabian lands as the luckiest of all good luck charms.

178

Next day, the Princess Ayesha decided to test Ahmad to find if he had indeed forsaken his spendthrift ways. She sent him a message, asking him if he would buy a new suit before he visited her in the Harem. To her delight, he replied that he had plenty of clothes of a style suitable to visit her and he was not going to buy anything more unless he really needed it. This set her mind at rest and she realised that the spell had certainly done its work.

She sat down and wrote to her father, asking him to come to the wedding and begging his forgiveness for running away. She told him that she was going to marry Ahmad out of true love for him and not just because he had rescued her from the tower.

Two months later, her father arrived in time for the wedding festivities. In his turn, he begged his daughter's forgiveness for imprisoning her in the tower to avoid giving offence to King Suliman (upon whom be peace).

No sooner had Ayesha's father spoken thus when a flock of white doves appeared out of the sky and settled on the palace roof. There they remained, cooing the while, until the marriage contracts were signed.

As the happy couple and guests sat down to the wedding feast, the doves flew in through the windows and dropped rose-petals on all the company.

Everyone marvelled as they flew away, but Ahmad and Ayesha knew that they were but bringing wedding congratulations from the Great King of Magicians, Suliman, Son of David (upon whom be peace!), whose creatures and messengers they undoubtedly were. And Sultan Ahmad used his treasure for the good of his people, becoming as well-loved as his father before him. He never wasted another coin during the rest of his long life, and Allah sent the couple many sons.

Maroof, the Cobbler Of Cairo

Once upon a time there lived in the city of Cairo, a cobbler named Maroof who made a living by patching boots and sandals. He had a very bad-tempered, ugly, mean, spiteful and worthless wife called Fatima who made his life a misery. She was forever scolding him, belittling him to everyone and calling down curses upon his head for being poor and thus having ruined her life. In fact, some of his friends thought it would have been better for him had he taken a cup of poison on his wedding day.

Often, he thought of taking another wife, younger and prettier, but he knew he could not afford one; nor would any other woman have lived under the same roof as Fatima for more than a few hours. But he was a quiet and patient man and he prayed that some day he might be relieved of her company by one of the Great Miracles of Allah, the Compassionate, the Merciful.

One day, Fatima said to him, "Bring me a vermicelli-cake soaked in honey from the bazaar. Mind you get it, or I will scratch your eyes out!"

Poor Maroof had not one dirham in his pocket, nor under his floor where other shop-keepers usually hid their cash, so he sent a heartfelt prayer to Heaven saying, "Oh Allah, vouchsafe me the price of the kunafah (cake) which Fatima wants, for I greatly value my eyesight, O Lord of the Worlds!"

All day he waited in his shop but nobody came and at the end of the day, he had not earned a single miserable coin. On his way home, he passed the baker's display of fine bread and cakes with a heavy heart.

The baker, seeing the cobbler's sad face, asked, "What is the matter, friend Maroof? Is your wife dead, that you look so glum?" and he almost doubled up with laughter because he knew how dreadfully Fatima bullied poor Maroof.

"No, I am in real trouble. I dread going back to tell her that I have not bought the kunafah which she ordered me to bring."

"I will give you some," said the cheerful baker. "Tell me how much you want, and you shall have it." He got out the cake tray and began to weigh out some of the delicious confection. Maroof thanked him with tears in his eyes but insisted on paying him for the cake as soon as he had the money.

"But," said the baker, "I have no honey to put on it. There is only cane syrup left. Will that be all right for you?"

"May Allah extend your days," cried Maroof, "I will take a pound of that; it is all the wretched Fatima deserves. She is lucky to get anything at all!"

So the baker wrapped it for him and Maroof went home with a light step. When he came in, his wife got off the sofa where she had been lounging and asked, "Where is the cake I ordered this morning?" Her narrow, lined face was screwed up with annoyance, ready for him to say that he had forgotten.

Maroof put the cake on the table and said, "Here it is! I was lucky that the baker gave me this free until I can pay, for I made not one coin today. There was no honey left though, so it is soaked in cane syrup instead."

"What?" screeched Fatima, "Do you seriously expect me to eat kunafah with cane syrup instead of honey? Wretched man, you treat me like a dog, I will not stand it! I could have married a rich man and eaten cake every day, instead of being begrudged every bite by a penniless cobbler!"

Maroof tried to remonstrate with her but it was useless. She took the cake and threw it at the wall, screaming so loudly that the family next door thought he was beating her. The cobbler managed to doze off for a few hours after she fell asleep exhausted. Next day, he opened up his shop with high hopes of earning some money to pay for the cake, at least.

But at midday, when he was busy mending a pair of old sandals, two men entered and took him before the Kadi, the local Magistrate: "What do you mean, wicked man, by beating your wife Fatima, so badly that she came in here to complain?"

"I did not touch her!" cried Maroof, "I am innocent!"

"Your wife's face was covered with blood when she came to my court," said the Kadi, "and so I believed her."

"In the Name of Allah, who shall be my Judge, I swear I never touched her!" repeated the distraught Maroof.

Now the Kadi being a wise and understanding man, said, "Well, go in peace and pray, buy your wife a honey cake. Here is the money. Make her happy and maybe there will be no more to quarrel about."

Maroof did as the Kadi had suggested but it was useless.

Next day, the Kadi's men came again and said that his wife had accused him of knocking out her tooth and she had the tooth in her hand to prove it. But Fatima's behaviour in court, screeching and pulling out her hair hysterically, did her case no good. Maroof was able to prove to the Kadi that she was lying, for the Kadi was a just man and could see what Maroof had to endure.

The Kadi dismissed both of them from his court and told them never to return.

The very next day, a friend came to Maroof and said, "Brother, hide yourself somewhere, for your wife has laid a complaint against you in the High Court and if she manages to convince the judges there, you will be in real trouble."

Convinced that he must flee, Maroof sold the lasts and other tools of his trade and got five silver pieces for them. Then he fled from the city through the Gate of Victory, the Bab-al-Nasr. It was the winter season and as he went, the heavy rains soon soaked him to the skin.

In a desolate spot, he came to a mound with a half-ruined house on it and tried to find shelter within. He raised his eyes to Heaven and cried: "Oh Allah, I beseech thee, have mercy! Let me find some way to escape from Fatima so that I shall not be tortured by her again!"

No sooner had he uttered these words, than a gigantic being appeared before him and said in a voice of thunder: "Who dares to come to this place to interrupt my rest - I, who have lain undisturbed in this cell for two hundred years?"

Maroof, his hair on end in terror, stammered out his sorry tale.

When he had finished, the Geni said, "Get up onto my shoulders and I will take you to another country, for your story moves me."

Maroof did as he was bid and in a few moments the Geni rose into the sky, high above Cairo and flew far, far away. At last they descended and the amazed cobbler found himself outside the gates of a great city, full of golden-domed buildings and tall, shimmering towers.

"Your wife will never find you here," said the Geni and disappeared.

Maroof entered the strange city, marvelling at all he saw. Seeing him clad in garments quite strange to the city, a man came up to him and asked him whence he came.

"I am from Cairo," Maroof replied.

The man said, "Then you must have been a year on the way, for that is the time it takes to go from here to Cairo."

"No, no," said Maroof, "I was only a short time flying here..."

The crowd which had gathered laughed him to scorn, thinking him a terrible liar.

While this was going on, a merchant riding a mule and with two black servants, heard the altercation and cried, "Cease this baiting of a stranger and show him a little respect!" To Maroof he said, "Oh my brother, will you come home with me? I will be your benefactor."

Gratefully the cobbler went with him, for he was feeling tired, hungry and very bewildered.

They arrived at a spacious house, richly-adorned and

furnished fit for a king. Maroof was given a room, where there were rich hangings and wonderful garments laid out for him. After a bath, he changed into clean clothes and joined the merchant for a wonderful meal of rich and exotic foods.

"What is your name?" asked his new friend, and the cobbler answered "I am Maroof, the Cobbler of Cairo, and I am escaping from my wife, Fatima, for she has become a dreadful enemy. They would not believe that I left Cairo and came here so fast but it is true, I swear it. A Geni or an Efrit brought me on his shoulders. It is all true, by Allah who must have heard my prayers!"

"I believe you," said the other, "I am Ali, the merchant and I will tell you what I shall do: I will give you a mule and two black boys. Tomorrow, you shall ride forth to the Merchants' Bazaar.

Then I will come and meet you at the coffee house and greet you, calling you by name and asking after your health, kissing you on the shoulder as if we were old friends."

He thought awhile before continuing: "Then, I will ask you if you have this or that kind of rich material - and you must answer that you have, and plenty of it. The other merchants will then question me about you, and I will tell them that you are completely to be trusted."

Ali the Merchant went on: "I will tell them that you are a man of generosity and of great wealth - and I shall lend you a purse with a thousand dinars so that you can flaunt it and, if a beggar comes to you, you can give him a princely sum.

In this way, your reputation as a rich merchant will be established, and good luck will assuredly come to you soon. That," concluded Ali, "is the way to become established in this city."

"Allah requite you for your generosity, most wonderful friend!" cried Maroof and could scarcely believe how his luck had changed even when the merchant handed him the heavy purse containing a thousand dinars.

The next day it all fell out as Ali had arranged. The merchant greeted him as an old friend at the coffee house in the bazaar and bade him sit with the other merchants as they discussed their business.

"Have you linen damask and finest Chinese silk?" Ali asked.

"Certainly, plenty of it," replied Maroof.

"Have you any of the yellow broad-cloth?" asked another merchant.

"Plenty!" replied Maroof.

"And any of the finest wool, the gazelle's-blood red variety?" asked a third.

"Plenty!" responded Maroof.

A poor beggar came by and each merchant gave him a few copper coins, but Maroof pulled out his money and gave him a gold piece. Knowing glances were exchanged and one or two murmured what was in the minds of all: "This merchant must indeed be a very rich man to give a beggar a piece of gold!"

Then, another beggar came, this time a poor old woman, and he gave her a golden coin too. One by one the beggars came, having quickly heard about the generosity of the strange merchant, until he had given away almost the entire fortune that Ali the Merchant had handed him.

"Would that I had another thousand to give to these wretched unfortunates," cried Maroof, "so that I could alleviate their condition until my baggage-camels come!"

After that, when they all assembled at the mosque for prayers, he borrowed five thousand dinars from a merchant and gave them all away.

"When my camels come, I will repay," he said grandly and went on distributing largesse. Ali the Merchant took him aside and said, "O Maroof, you are becoming very high-handed with other peoples' money! Did I tell you to do all this borrowing? Be careful and stop borrowing, for those who borrow must repay, you know!"

"Don't worry," said Maroof, "when my camels come, I will repay every debt!"

"What!" shouted Ali. "Have you camels coming?"

"Plenty!" said Maroof calmly, feeling in his pocket as yet another beggar approached.

"By Allah and the Invisible Controls!" cried Ali with feeling. "Did I teach you this ritual that you should repeat it to ME? I tell you, Maroof, I am extremely angry!"

"Leave it all to me," retorted Maroof loftily. "My camels are on the way and as soon as they come I will pay back everyone as I have promised. Do you take me for a cheat?" and he drew himself up proudly.

Ali went away and after three weeks had passed the other merchants came to him asking, "When are we going to get our money? Your friend does nothing but throw it away on all the rogues and vagabonds in the street .... and his camels have not yet come!"

"He owes me a thousand dinars too," said Ali mournfully, "I thought he would start trading properly instead of this insane behaviour. Go, complain of him to the King, for he has imposed upon all of us."

They went to the King and complained of Maroof's behaviour and told how he now owed them vast sums, having pretended that camels loaded with immense wealth were on their way.

Now, the King of that country was a very mean and covetous man. When he heard of the great generosity of which Maroof, the foreign merchant was capable - having given away to beggars some sixty thousand gold pieces in the space of twenty-one days - he said to his Grand Vizier, "If this merchant were not a man of tremendous wealth in reality, he would certainly not be giving all this money away like this. His caravan must be coming and the merchants are only jealous of him. Invite him to the Palace for I intend to join his wealth to mine by giving him my daughter in marriage - he sounds just right for her!" At this, the Grand Vizier was seized with a fit of coughing - he had always hoped that the Princess Dunya would one day be his.

Maroof was brought before the King, who said to him, "The merchants of this city say that you owe them such-and-such a sum. Why have you kept them waiting twenty-one days for what is their due?"

Maroof laughed and said, "Oh King, my camels will come laden with treasure far beyond these paltry sums, which I have given to the poor. Then I will repay those who lent me anything, double if that will satisfy them."

Then the King sought to test Maroof by handing him a rare

jewel for which he had paid a huge amount, saying, "Can you price this for me, Maroof and tell me its true worth?" Maroof took the jewel, which broke between his finger and thumb.

"By Allah," cried the King, "you have broken my jewel!"

"This is no jewel," said Maroof. "It is but a piece of worthless coloured glass, otherwise it would not have broken like this. Besides, it is only the size of an almond. I call a jewel a jewel when it is the size of a walnut!"

"And have you jewels of that size in your camel train?" asked the greedy King.

"Plenty of them!" replied Maroof and the avaricious monarch asked, "Will you give me jewels of that size when your camels come?"

Maroof replied, "Plenty and Your Majesty shall have them all without charge!"

Thereupon the King told all the merchants to go home and that he himself would pay them when Maroof's caravan arrived.

The Grand Vizier said to the King, "O King of the Age! Can we trust this man for I cannot quite believe all he says..."

"Yes, yes," responded the potentate. "He is perfectly straight-forward; he obviously has more than I could ever hope to have unless I ally myself with him. Talk to him about the Princess Dunya and offer him her hand in marriage, for I must have him and all his goods at my disposal."

So, very reluctantly, the Grand Vizier went to Maroof and said, "The King has taken a liking to you and wants you to take his daughter, Princess Dunya, in marriage. She is very beautiful and a much sought-after lady."

"Oh no," said Maroof, "I cannot think of marriage until my camels arrive, as the dowries of king's daughters are likely to be vast and I have nothing at the moment. I will need about five thousand purses of gold as the bride's portion, another thousand purses to distribute to the poor on the wedding night and a further thousand for those who will walk in the wedding procession. And yet more will be needed to provide presents of money for the troops guarding us."

Much relieved, the Grand Vizier returned and told the King.

But the king said, "Here is a man who both refuses gifts from others and yet is so generous himself - how can such a man be any sort of imposter? Go and fetch him here and I will make the arrangements with him myself. After all, it is a father's duty to see to the true happiness of his daughter."

When Maroof arrived, the King began at once, "You shall not put me off with excuses. I have plenty in my own treasury. Take these keys and help yourself, I beg you. About my daughter's dowry, I will happily leave that until your camels come and you can give what you wish to her then."

The Shaykh-al-Islam (the religious head of the community) was requested to make out the royal marriage contract between Maroof and the Princess Dunya. For the wedding festivities, the city was decorated from end to end with lights and flags. Performers who could swallow swords and eat fire jostled with small boys conjuring with oranges. Men led dancing bears on chains, drummers drummed, pipers played merry tunes, dancers whirled like spinning tops and everywhere there was joy and merriment.

But the Grand Vizier ground his teeth as Maroof sent again and again to the Royal Treasury for more to shower upon the troubadours, clowns, gypsies and dancers. The celebrations went on for forty days and nights.

On the forty-first day Maroof, scattering money all the way, was led by the happy courtiers to the Princess Dunya's private apartments in the Palace.

Then Maroof said to her, "I am most ashamed that your royal father has caught me unprepared like this, without money or jewels to lavish upon you as I would dearly love to do."

But the beautiful Princess Dunya stopped his mouth with her hand and said "When your camels come, you shall give me what you wish, my dear husband." Then they happily greeted each other as man and wife.

Next day Maroof, dressing himself in his finest, went to the Emirs and Viziers and, after discussions ranging over all the affairs of State, he presented them with large sums of money as tokens of his esteem. This went on for a further twenty days after the magnificent wedding festivities had ended.

189

The Chief Treasurer went to the King and said "Your Majesty, may you live for ever! The Treasury is now in grave danger of being emptied completely. In fact, there is only enough money left for about another ten days. Your son-in-law's baggage train had better come soon or else there will be nothing left to buy food, even for those here in the Palace."

The King was distressed beyond measure and sent for the Grand Vizier. "If this man is an imposter and your lovely daughter's beauty has been sold for nothing, then we shall have to punish him with the utmost severity!" said the Grand Vizier, scarcely troubling to conceal his satisfaction.

"How are we learn the truth now?" asked the King.

"No-one can more easily wheedle out a man's secrets than his wife," said the jealous Vizier. "Send for the Princess and let us tell her what we suspect. She can ask him herself."

"So be it," agreed the King.

When Princess Dunya arrived, her father and the Grand Vizier told her their suspicions and got her to agree to question her husband that very night - and to inform them next day.

So before they went to sleep, the Princess asked Maroof, almost as if in a dreamy state, "Tell me, dearest husband, what is the truth about your financial condition? Is there in reality a priceless caravan of jewels and silks coming, or is it all just a fantasy?"

"My dear wife," said he, "I must confess that there is no caravan. I am really Maroof, the Cobbler from Cairo, who had to flee from my ugly, unpleasant shrew of a wife, Fatima, and I beg you to forgive me."

At that, the Princess laughed and said, "My dear husband, I will try to help you! My father's Vizier has long suspected you and persuaded my father to ask me to find out the truth tonight. But I will not betray you. Do now as I say. Go and put on a Mameluke's garb and ride away from here as fast as you may. Here is a purse of five thousand dinars; go and become a merchant in another country and let me know where you are one day. Go quickly before the dawn!"

So, dressing in the long robe of one of the King's White

Slaves, the Mamelukes, he took a horse and was able to ride out of the city unrecognised.

Next morning, the King sent for his daughter and asked what she had found out about Maroof. The Grand Vizier too was there waiting to hear that Maroof was an imposter.

"Oh, Royal Father," said the Princess Dunya, "this morning, just as dawn was approaching, a messenger came with dreadful news. After fighting bravely, many of the White Mamelukes who were in charge of my husband's camel-train were butchered by bandits, who fell upon them in a lonely pass. There were many wounded and most of the baggage-camels laden with goods have been driven off by the attackers. My husband rose at once and rode off to be with his Mamelukes. He plans to regroup the caravan and bring it here as soon as he can." So saying, she went back to her own apartments, smiling behind her veil.

The King and the Grand Vizier believed her of course and the King, despite his greed, felt rather sorry for his son-in-law. The Vizier however, was glad he had gone and devoutly hoped that he would never return.

Maroof meanwhile, rode until he arrived in the neighbouring country and, being very hungry, went up to a peasant who was ploughing a small piece of land. "Peace be upon you," began Maroof.

"And upon you be peace," was the rejoinder. "Are you one of the Sultan's Mamelukes, my Lord?"

"Yes," replied Maroof. "Is there a town nearby where I might buy some provisions and stable my horse?"

"I will go and bring food for you and the horse from my village," said the man. "For you will have to ride a long way yet to get to the nearest town."

"Thank you," said Maroof. "Meanwhile I will carry on with your ploughing." Maroof dismounted and, tying his horse's reins to a tree, walked to the field.

As he started to move the bulls which were pulling the plough, something seemed to catch in the ploughshare and he stopped them to clear it. His fingers found a heavy ring attached to an alabaster slab sticking out of the earth. He pulled at the ring with both hands and it moved, bringing up the alabaster slab and disclosing a flight of steps underneath! Maroof went down the steps until he came to a large room lit by an eerie greenish light. This room was filled with blocks of gold from floor to ceiling; walking through it he came to another room - this one was filled with emeralds, rubies, opals and diamonds! There were sacks overflowing with the jewels. Going through another door, he found a third room in which there was only a crystal chest and within it, clearly visible, was a golden coffer.

"I wonder what there is in that?" he thought. He opened it and found inside a seal-ring of gold on which there were engraved strange symbols. He rubbed the ring to see them better and at once he heard a loud voice which said "I am here, O Master. Order it and it shall be yours! Whatever you require, it shall be done." A huge Geni stood before him with folded arms.

"Who are you?" asked Maroof.

"I am the Slave of this seal-ring which you are wearing, my Lord, and I serve whoever wears it. Lo, you have become the Master of this ring and I am your slave. If you want to raze a city to the ground, or raise one to the skies; kill a king, or make one; unlock that which is sealed or seal that which you want hidden, bid me. But.... beware of rubbing the ring twice in succession, for then you will eliminate me and I shall be consumed with the fire of the names engraved on the ring. Thus you might lose me when you needed me most!"

Maroof wondered if he were dreaming - "And what is your name, O Slave of the Ring ?" he asked.

"My name is Abualsadat," said the apparition.

"O Abualsadat," said Maroof, "What is this place and who put you in this casket?"

"O my Lord, this is the Hoard of Shaddad and I was his slave while he yet lived."

"Can you bring this treasure out of the ground?" asked Maroof.

"Yes, indeed I can," said the Geni and summoned a large number of handsome boys with golden baskets, who carried the jewels and gold out in no time at all.

"Whose are these workers?" asked Maroof. "There are hundreds of them."

"Master, they are my sons and are here to serve you in any capacity you may wish - as servants or as animals. They will be honoured to assist you."

"Then," said Maroof, "let some of them be turned into mules, so that they can carry this treasure away and others into muleteers, so that I can have a mule-train greater than any in the whole world."

"Your word is my command!" responded the Geni and within the blink of an eye, seven hundred of the boys changed into strong mules with panniers full of treasure and another hundred took the shapes of slaves. Others took the semblance of fine saddle-horses with flowing manes and tails and yet others appeared as camels with bales of costly stuffs bulging from sacks piled high on their backs.

Just when the whole caravan was ready to depart, there arrived the peasant who had gone for provisions, with a dish of lentils for Maroof and a small nose-bag of oats for the horse.

Maroof greeted him warmly and shared the lentils with him. Though puzzled by the tremendous caravan of camels, horses and mules which reached as far as the eye could see, the peasant sat down and ate with him. When they were finished, Maroof filled the dish with gold pieces and handed it to the man saying, "Take this with you to your village and buy what you may require, for I am indebted to you."

The peasant returned to his village driving his bulls before him, overjoyed at his good fortune and well pleased with the gold.

"Now," said Maroof, "I wish to return to the country of my father-in-law and show him my baggage-train, for it is now as I had pictured it to him and his Grand Vizier!"

The Geni, sent ahead clad as a courtier, flew to the palace of Maroof's father-in-law just as the Grand Vizier was saying to the King, "I told you, Your Majesty, that he was dishonest and deceitful! He has made his escape, whatever the Princess Dunya may say..."

The Geni appeared with a letter and prostrated himself before the King saying, "Your Majesty, I bring a letter from your son-in-law. Here it is."

The King broke open the seal and read: "Most Respected King, I have now settled my affairs with my enemies, rescued my followers and brought as much of my treasure as the bandits have left me. However, I think that sufficient is left to pay off all my debts and hold my head up for the rest of my life."

The Princess, coming in at that instant, heard her father reading this aloud and her eyes shone with excitement, knowing that Maroof had triumphed.

"Where is your master now?" the Grand Vizier asked the Geni, who was still standing respectfully in front of the throne, dressed as a courtier.

"He should be here by tomorrow at the latest," replied the Geni, "and his caravan of treasure with him."

Princess Dunya was delighted and giving a cry of joy returned to her apartments to have her hair washed and perfumed so that she could dress in all her finery and be ready to welcome her husband home in a fitting manner.

"Permanent glory, victory and long life to Your Majesty!" intoned the Geni, who was enjoying himself behaving as a courtier, and he backed out of the room.

"Allah blacken your brow, Vizier!" shouted the King. "How often have you besmirched my good son-in-law's name with suspicion ever since he came here?"

He ordered his troops out to accompany Maroof back into the city with his baggage-train. The news ran like wildfire through all the bazaars and people said to each other, "The baggage-train of the King's son-in-law is coming at last. Now everyone will see the wonders that he has brought!"

Ali the Merchant heard the news and said to himself: "This must be some sort of trick. Can this really be Maroof the Cobbler, who escaped from his shrewish wife, Fatima, in Cairo and borrowed all those thousands of dinars in my name? This is something I really must see." So he joined the crowds gathering to welcome Maroof home.

The Geni, Abualsadat, reported to Maroof the preparations for his reception and the tremendous excitement at the news of his return. Maroof dressed specially for the occasion in a suit sewn with the finest gems with a turban made of the most beautiful silk, decorated with an egret's feather in a golden brooch. He lay on a silken litter carried by four of the Geni's sons.

As he entered the city at the head of his caravan, it passed Ali the Merchant and his friends. The merchants' eyes were bulging and Ali was thinking,"What a deception, O King of Imposters! I fear that those bags will turn out to contain only bricks!" for he still could not believe in Maroof's fortune.

As he neared the Royal Palace, the King arose from his throne and went out to meet him and embraced him.

Entering the Palace, Maroof gave orders to his slaves: "Select the best gems and take them to his noble Majesty. Take the remainder to the Royal Treasury, except for this treasure-casket of jewels and these bales of silken materials which are for the Princess Dunya. Ask her to distribute what she wishes among her handmaidens. Tell her that I will be with her later on, when I find some special gifts I have for her."

First, he paid out all the merchants to whom he owed money, double the amount they had lent him as he had promised. Fine presents were given to each of the Emirs and Viziers of his father-in-law's Court. Then he distributed alms to the poor and needy in great quantity.

Meanwhile Ali the Merchant marvelled and said to himself, "I wonder what sort of swindle it was that Maroof worked to accumulate so much treasure?"

Then the slaves came to Maroof and said, "The vaults of the Royal Treasury are now full. Where shall we put the rest of the gold?"

Maroof said, "Give it in handfuls to the troops, for they have guarded us well on the last lap of the journey." And all was done as he asked.

When he saw so much being given away, the King said, "But... but... is this not rather too generous?"

Maroof laughed and said, "There is more when I need it," and so there was, because of the power of the ring.

Meanwhile, the Princess Dunya, overjoyed to see Maroof back

195

again, decked herself with beautiful jewels from the casket which he had given her. She was curious though, saying to herself, "I wish I knew how he came by all that wealth. It could not be from trading with the five thousand dinars I gave him."

When Maroof went in to greet his wife she pretended to tease him saying, "Were you mocking me when you told me that you were a poor cobbler and a fugitive from your shrewish, old wife? No-one could be dearer to me, whether you be rich or poor, good or bad, once-married or thrice-married! But I would like you to tell me why you said those words."

Maroof replied, "My dear, I was merely testing your loyalty to see if you would stand by me whatever I said. But now I know that you really love me and I thank Allah for it!" Almost shyly he added, "Wait here for a moment."

Then he withdrew and, rubbing the ring, said, "O Abualsadat, I want a dress sewn with gems for my dear wife and a necklace of forty unique jewels."

"To hear is to obey!" responded the Geni and, in a twinkling, placed the necklace and dress in Maroof's hands. Maroof took them to the Princess Dunya and presented them to her.

She was excited beyond measure and, calling her maidens, she arrayed herself in the new finery. Looking in Maroof's treasure-casket, she discovered earrings, bracelets and rings to match the necklace. Attired thus, she went forth to Maroof, looking every inch a queen.

But, alas, for too much splendour!

When her father saw her dressed thus in new garments, day-after-day with handmaidens clad in like manner, the covetous King began to wonder at the source of his son-in-law's wealth. He said to the Grand Vizier, "Go to my son-in-law's garden one evening and ply him with wine. When the wits are out of his head with drink, see if he has a secret. He could be some kind of bandit chief."

The Grand Vizier was delighted to be given the task and looked forward very much to prising Maroof's secret from him in this way - whatever it might be .

Meanwhile a servant came to the King saying: "Your Majesty,

the horses, mules and servants which made up your son-in-law's caravan have disappeared. There were seven hundred mules, to say nothing of their grooms, their horses and camels. When we had prepared their fodder, we sought them but they had gone! No-one saw them go!"

"How can this be?" exclaimed the King, "and why? When my son-in-law comes out of the Harem tell him about this."

But Maroof just smiled and said, "Oh well, they had to go sometime; why should they remain? Their work was done."

He knew, of course, that they had simply returned to the realm of the Slave of the Ring, whose creatures they were.

But the King and the Grand Vizier were more puzzled than ever at Maroof's attitude: "What sort of a man is this who does not care if hundreds of beasts and servants vanish into thin air overnight?"

The King and his Vizier decided forthwith to invite Maroof to dine with them in a beautiful garden, sweetly scented and alive with songbirds. Maroof accepted willingly, suspecting nothing, and they went there the same afternoon.

In the garden was a beautiful pavilion, lit by lanterns, where they sat and talked. The Vizier told one story after another and with tall tales, merry quips and amusing incidents, the afternoon passed pleasantly. A huge meal was carried in on golden trays from the Royal kitchens. After dinner, they were served with ice-cold sherbets, but the wily Vizier had laced Maroof's drink with a powerful drug. Presently, his mind began to wander till he could not tell left from right. This was the moment!

"Tell us if you will," the Vizier cajoled, "how you come by these enormous riches. You must be either a King or a supernatural being to have such a wealth of marvellous possessions. Do you receive them from some secret source?"

Poor Maroof, now quite befuddled and out of his wits, confided in the King and the Grand Vizier the magical properties of his golden seal-ring. In his bemused state, he even pulled off the ring and handed it to the Vizier, shouting, "Is it not exquisite? Look at the magical engravings on it!"

"If I rub it, will the Slave appear?" asked the Vizier, putting on

197

the ring while the King looked on.

The Slave of the Ring appeared, for the Grand Vizier had rubbed it; through his stupor, Maroof heard him say, "Take this wretch and drop him into the most desolate part of Arabia, the Empty Quarter, so that he may die of hunger and thirst!"

The Geni obeyed and carried Maroof on his back till they reached the desolate region known as the Empty Quarter, where he set him down.

"Why are you doing this to me, Abualsadat?" cried Maroof. "I thought I was your master."

"As I told you, I am the Slave of whoever possesses the ring," replied the Geni and flew off, leaving Maroof to curse his stupidity and sink to the ground in horror, lamenting his fate.

Back in the garden, the King said to the Grand Vizier, "Let me have the ring now, so that I too can make a wish."

But the Vizier shouted at him, "Am I such a fool as to give you this wonderful ring now that I have got it myself? No! With it, I shall become King in your stead!" and he rubbed the ring once more.

Again Abualsadat appeared and the Vizier ordered, "Take this wretched King to the same Empty Quarter where you have put his son-in-law, so they can mingle their tears together!"

"I hear and obey," was the reply. And when the King and his son-in-law were together, they did indeed mingle their tears.

The Grand Vizier now got himself up in his finest garments and with the ring on his finger, called the Court together and announced: "With this ring, I can send you all into the wilderness, as I have done with the King and his son-in-law! Unless you acknowledge me as King forthwith, who knows what I might not do!"

When the courtiers saw his wild eyes and heard the purpose in his voice, what could they do but elect him as their ruler.

Then the evil Grand Vizier sent a message to the Princess Dunya to the effect that he was going to take her as his wife and that she should prepare herself to accept him. He was now master of the Ring which was the source of Maroof's wealth and, with its help, he had banished both her husband and her father to the Empty Quarter. Also, he had always been passionately in love with her.

Princess Dunya was determined to resist him. She sent word that he must allow her a period of mourning and then she would see him - she was now grieving for both her father and her husband.

But the Grand Vizier demanded to see her that very night and would neither acknowledge a period of mourning nor brook any delay. Princess Dunya realised that the Vizier's head had been turned by the limitless wealth and power which he now commanded. She agreed to receive him therefore and worked out a plan to deceive him.

After eating and drinking with the courtiers and boasting of his conquest, the Grand Vizier - who was now the King - went to her apartments. Coming forth with all her maidens, the Princess Dunya bowed low before him saying, "O, how kind you are to come to me here instead of sending for me. Now I can entertain you royally! See, I have put on all my jewels for you and my finest caftan!"

The Vizier's suspicions were lulled by her words and her smiles but as he came close to her, she screamed, "Oh, I cannot bear to see the Slave of the Ring looking at me like that! Quick! Take off the ring and throw it into the corner of the room!"

"Is the Slave of the Ring watching us?" bellowed the Vizier. "How dare he? I will soon get rid of him!" He took the ring off his finger and threw it into a corner.

Adroitly, the Princess caught the ring, put it on her own finger and rubbed it. When the Slave of the Ring appeared, she said, "Take this villain and lock him into the deepest dungeon and bring me the key. Then bring back my father, the King, and my dear husband from wherever you took them."

The Geni answered, "Mistress, I hear and obey!"

In less time than it takes to tell, he had alighted beside Maroof and the King. He lifted them up onto his shoulders and flew swiftly back to the Palace. The Princess Dunya wept with relief and told them what she had done with the wicked Vizier.

When all three were somewhat restored and refreshed,

Princess Dunya pleaded with her father: "Please make Maroof your Grand Vizier and let that villainous man rot in the dungeon. He would have become my husband this very night had I not tricked him out of the ring."

The King agreed and Maroof was overjoyed. He praised his wife's brains as well as her beauty.

The King said, "Well, now that is settled, please give the ring either to me or to your husband."

"No," said the Princess, "I will keep the ring, for neither of you would use it properly. Anything that you wish for, you shall ask of me and I will request it from the Slave of the Ring. After my death, you can choose which of you is to have it."

The two men had little choice but to agree to her wishes, so they left it at that.

For some time things went on very happily. Then her father died and Princess Dunya made Maroof, King in her father's place. A son was born to them, a most beautiful child, but when the young prince was only seven years old, Queen Dunya fell ill and knew she was going to die.

She gave the ring to her husband and said, "Maroof, be careful with this wonderful seal-ring and take great care of our son, for many things can happen if you do not guard a magical object as powerful as this one. Remember its power......."

Maroof promised to be careful of the Prince and the ring; and Queen Dunya died next day.

When Queen Dunya's funeral and the period of mourning were over, Maroof bethought himself of the peasant who had been the instrument of his finding the ring and subsequent good fortune. He sent for him and made him Vizier so that the man and his family enjoyed every privilege.

One night Maroof went to bed, looking forward to taking his son on a hunting expedition the next day. Suddenly, in the middle of the night he felt someone beside him and drew away, thinking he was having a nightmare. But an old woman sat up in bed beside him and said, "Do you not know me, dear husband? I am Fatima, your wife from Cairo!"

"From Cairo?" he cried, "How did you find me here? It is

eight years since I left; I had forgotten all about you!"

"So it would seem," replied Fatima coyly. "It is a long story. After you had gone away, I began to realise what a good husband you had been. I wept for many a night afterwards and tried everywhere to find you. Having no money, I had to become a beggar on the streets and so I continued for years. Then, last night, I repented of how I had used you all our married life and was ashamed and cried 'Oh, would that I could see my dear husband again and ask him to forgive me!'

Suddenly, a supernatural being appeared before me and asked 'Woman, why do you weep and cry out like this night after night, year after year?' 'Because I am truly sorry,' I sobbed, 'and wish to see my husband again.'

'What is your husband's name?' said the being.

'Maroof,' I answered.

'There is a King Maroof, who rules a distant land,' said the apparition. 'I will take you to him at once.'

'I am willing to go anywhere, if I can only make amends,' I cried, and he took me up on his shoulders and we flew high above the clouds where there is neither day nor night and at last I found myself here beside you. Praise be to Allah that I am reunited with you!"

Maroof, awoken out of sleep, was not sure whether he was now awake or dreaming: "Meanwhile, I married a second time," he found himself saying, "and I have a young son, seven years old. I am the Ruler here and I have a wonderful slave who will bring me anything I desire if I but rub this ring. His name is Abualsadat. I only have to ask him and anything can be mine. So, if you wish to return home, I can have you transported there and give you a fine palace, choice silks and wonderful jewels and enough money to keep you in comfort for the rest of your life."

"I want to stay here with you," she pleaded and kissed his hands, vowing eternal repentance. So, in the end, he had a separate palace built for her and gave her many slaves to do her bidding, everything in fact, that a Queen might possess.

But she looked upon the son of Queen Dunya with hatred, because he was not her own son. Every time she saw him she became more jealous.

The boy, for his part, disliked his stepmother and, each time he saw her, he hated her the more. Maroof meanwhile was occupied with affairs of state. He avoided Fatima as much as he could, for she had grown uglier than ever, grizzled, stringy and wrinkled.

Moreover, her nature had not changed despite her new life of luxury. She was mischievous and deceitful and not at all repentant: now in addition she was jealous of Maroof's good luck.

One night, Fatima arose from her bed, determined to search for the ring, the source of all Maroof's wealth. She tiptoed into the King's bedchamber and began to look everywhere, hoping to take it off his finger while he slept and make herself Queen.

Now, Maroof had been out with friends for most of the night and had left his seal-ring behind on a cushion, so that it could not be taken from him as it had been, once before.

As luck would have it, the young Prince was not asleep and saw his wicked stepmother creeping about. He followed her as she went into his father's bedroom. In his hand the boy had a short, sharp sword which he had been given for his birthday, as strong and as sharp as a real one. Often Maroof had laughed at him when he strutted about with it saying, "And whom do you think you will be able to slay with that, my boy?"

The child answered boldly, "Father, it will not fail to cut off some head which deserves the cutting!"

At this moment of which we speak, the little Prince saw Fatima look down at Maroof lying asleep on his bed. With a hiss of excitement, she saw the ring on a cushion beside his bed.

In a trice, she had bent low to slip it onto her finger but before she could even rub it, the short sword of the young Prince descended upon her neck. Her head was severed from her body and Maroof awoke with a start as his son shouted out in triumph.

The ring flew off the woman's finger and landed at Maroof's feet. He picked it up with trembling fingers and put it on again. The Prince told his father what caused him to despatch the wicked Fatima to the Lower Regions and Maroof called for the slaves to remove the body for a proper burial.

He gave Fatima a huge funeral and she was buried under a

large slab of marble. This, he hoped, would keep her away from him for ever.

And so it did. Maroof lived happily with a third wife and enjoyed a long life, until the Sunderer of All Delights and the Settler of All Accounts took him to his rest, to await the Day of Judgement and Joyful Reunions.

Meanings of Words

Allah - God.
Bilquis - The Queen of Sheba (Sabah in Arabia).
Caftan - A robe.
Burnous - A cloak with attached hood, generally of woollen material.
Caliph - A ruler.
Caravan - String of camels laden with merchandise, or carrying pilgrims or travellers.
Dervish - A pious man, usually travelling from place to place.
Eblis - The Devil.
Efrit - Jinn.
Emir - A prince.
Geni/Jinn - A magical being.
Harem - Ladies' quarters.
Kadi - A magistrate, a judge.
Kismet - Fate, Destiny.
Koran - The Holy Book of Islam.
Mecca - The Holy City of Moslem Pilgrimage.
Mehari - A racing camel.
Mosque - Place of worship.
Oasis - Fertile part of the desert, generally with a well and palm trees.
Sheikh - Chief of a tribe, or a learned man.
Sultan - A king.
Sultana - A queen.
Souk - Bazaar or market.
Suliman - King of the Jinn (Solomon).
Taleb - Religious head or teacher.
Vizier - Court Adviser, Minister.

OTHER BOOKS FROM OCTAGON PRESS

TALES OF AFGHANISTAN
by Amina Shah

Stories from the author's ancestral home-
land, collected from servants and royal courts,
from teahouses and caravanserais these tales
told wherever storytellers gather, have been
passed down for generations in the East.

Here they are retold with that authentic magic
which will ensure their survival as stories for
children of all ages in the West.

THE ASSEMBLIES OF
AL-HARIRI
Retold by Amina Shah

Since the time of the First Crusade, the picaresque adventures of the rascal Abu Zaid of Saruj have been read, admired, imitated and praised, from Spain to the Hindu Kush.

Al-Hariri of Basra (1054-1122) is variously described as a silk merchant, a high official of the Seljuk monarch Malik Shah and the author of *The Assemblies:* regarded for eight centuries as the greatest treasure in Arabic literature after the Koran.

For Arabic-speakers, the book remains one of the greatest classics on how to use their language; for us the adventures of the astonishing rogue Abu Zaid are meat enough. But the real inner thread of this amazing book which makes it a world classic, is that the tales and events mirror the antics of the human mind in its way through life.

THE TALE OF THE FOUR DERVISHES
of Amir Khusru
Retold by Amina Shah

The Four Dervishes of the tale are searching for their hearts' desire: intricately woven into their stories are seemingly endless others ... of love and honour; steadfastness and treachery; of magic palaces and great idols; of kings and jinns; beautiful princesses and faithful servants; brave young princes and evil usurpers.

This allegory was recited when he was ill to the great 13th century Sufi teacher Nizamuddin Awliyya by his disciple Amir Khusru, the eminent Persian poet. On his recovery, Nizamuddin placed a benediction on the book and it is widely believed that the recitation of this story will restore health to the ailing.

Since the tale was translated into Urdu a century-and-a-half ago, it has been regarded as a classic of that language. Amina Shah's re-telling of it now enables its beauty and power to reach the English-speaking world.

THE GOLDEN CARAVAN
by Sirdar Ikbal Ali Shah

The whole flavour of the East is here: Hajis rub shoulders with Bolsheviks; Sultans with Sufis; Colonial officers with alchemists. You can visit Turkestan and Egypt, the Himalayas and the Khyber Pass, the world of the Hindu, the Moslem, the desert and the palace. From these tales authentically set in the cultures of the Near East, a different and often surprising world emerges, filled with magic and adventure.

ESCAPE FROM CENTRAL ASIA
by Sirdar Ikbal Ali Shah

Twenty gripping stories told with pace and humour, dovetailed with allegory. On a modern-day pilgrimage, several travellers entertain - and edify - each other in the classical manner.

These tales were written while the author was India's cultural representative for North Africa and Western Asia.

AFGHANISTAN OF THE AFGHANS
by Sirdar Ikbal Ali Shah

As well as folklore and traditional tales of heroes, this book covers the history, geography, customs, spells, charms, Sufism and religion of the country. Written by one of Afghanistan's major literary celebrities, it is a most readable account of the "God-gifted realm" of the Afghans and has been regarded as a standard work for over half a century.